Pathway to Christ

A Christian Workbook

Malachi Mitchell

PATHWAY TO CHRIST

First edition. April 3, 2024.

Copyright © 2024 Malachi Mitchell.

ISBN: 979-8224293476

Written by Malachi Mitchell.

Endorsements

"This book is a must-read for every Christian. It is filled with fundamental scriptural truths that challenge you to become who God wants you to be. On the journey to *becoming*, you will have the practical and spiritual tools to walk on the right path.

Pathway to Christ is a journey through the Word of God that will empower you to live your God-given purpose in Christ. It's not just a good read; it's an experience. A powerful, practical, and reliable resource that every person of faith needs!

This book is not just for reading but for studying and applying. It will increase your biblical knowledge, faith, and ability to experience God personally and intimately. You will be empowered to walk the pathway that leads to successful living in this life while preparing you for the glorious eternal one next."

Jessica Janniere

Speaker

Best-Selling Author, *My Colored World: A Memoir*

"Disoriented about your direction in life? Knowing God's purpose for you will reduce your stress & simplify your decisions, and you'll begin living on purpose with PURPOSE!

In Pathway to Christ, Malachi Mitchell answers some of life's most challenging and perplexing questions in simple Scriptural ways that will revolutionize your spiritual walk! It's time to fully arise, shine, and express your gifts and talents. This book will lead you to more significant influence and impact as its truth transforms you!

This is the hour to lead by purpose and passion. As you do, you'll exit mediocrity and come into Extraordinary Living! A groundbreaking book designed to walk you out of confusion into certainty & confidence straight into a life of significance!"

Dr. **R**oseanna **R**oman

Author | Tv Host | Speaker

Founder of Morning Manna & Kingdom Voice's Ministries

"Pathway to Christ " is a rare book that comes around occasionally, and it is a game changer to those who read and study the principles inside it. This **must-read** book will fill your soul with fundamental scriptural truths that will challenge you to become the person you were created to become.

Significantly, few books will inspire you in the way that Pathway to Christ does, to live your purpose-driven life and to live it the way God wants all of us to live it. This book is your GPS to help you live a fulfilled spiritual life."

Greg **W**alker

Speaker | Coach | Consultant

USA TODAY Best-Selling Author

Dream to Grow Rich: How to Dream ~ Grind ~ Hustle Your Way to Success

"The Pathway to Christ is an excellent resource tool and definitive guidebook for living a fulfilling and God-driven life. Let's be clear: this is a WORKBOOK, but it is more than that; it is an exploration into the soul of "man" as we struggle to grow in our walk with God. Malachi provides the reader with the practical tools and biblical resources to empower us to lead purpose-driven spiritual lives fortified by the Word of God.

The Pathway to Christ is a definitive resource and study guide for anyone seeking to grow in their understanding and knowledge of Christ's life and message; from those who are "new in Christ" to the experienced Biblical scholar, you will be touched and inspired by Bible-based teachings that Malachi offers. This is a seminal spiritual guidebook to building a spiritual foundation for our spiritual life journey. I highly recommend it!"

Ric **E**pps

Vice President, Academic Senate

Vice Chair, College Council

Professor

Political Science

Behavioral Science & Social Science Department

Imperial Valley College

richard.epps@imperial.edu

*One way to define spiritual
maturity is when you can study
differing doctrinal viewpoints
enough to understand how people
arrive at their conclusions.
You may not agree with their
conclusions, but at least you have
studied it with enough objectivity
to understand how they arrived at
their conclusions.*

~Richard Wayne Garganta

Table of Contents

Introduction

For as long as I can remember, learning about the Bible and how to live a life that God would be pleased with was something I was born into. When I first met both of my parents, they were Christians, God-fearing people. Dad is a Bishop and the senior pastor of the Good Samaritan Church of San Diego. As of the writing of this workbook, he has been in ministry for over 50 years and married to the same beautiful woman for over sixty-three blessed years. So, hearing about Christ was not strange in my early childhood because it was my way of life, my pathway. My parents talked about it, walked it, and taught the Bible at home and church.

Growing up, I loved camping. I can't figure out why because we never went camping! But during sixth-grade camp, I got a taste of the outdoors and the love of exploring the unknown. From then on, I just loved being outdoors. As children, my brother and I would be sent back to the country where our grandparents lived, Fairmead, California, for the whole summer. It was where my parents first met as children. I have great memories of walking through the fields and discovering the many different paths. It was one of my most incredible adventures as a child. We just never knew what we might find on one of those pathways. We used to hear so many scary stories while in the country and how, at night, the boogieman would walk those pathways looking for his next victim. It was fun but nerve-racking.

Many pathways in life hold the keys to success and failure. There is only one proper pathway that will grant you the success in life you desire. People have told us what pathways we should take for most of our lives. These pathways are not of our choosing but are the choice of those doing the dictating. When does it stop? When will it end? It won't! Not until you decide to stop listening to people whose pathways are not the pathways you desire to take. The Pathway to Christ shares a simple formula for choosing the right one. You will never be happy until you live the life you dreamed of, filled with people going in the same direction, accomplishing many of the same goals, and achieving the kind of success you long to achieve.

Get ready to read and embark upon a journey that will change not only your life as you read it but is guaranteed to change everyone else's life close to you. Often, people are unaware that their traveling pathway will never get them to their destination. The only way to get to the place you truly want to be is to get off the path you are on. Your GPS may be faulty, and you don't even realize it.

You will not find empty promises and unreachable goals in this workbook. This workbook is complete with what it takes to get on that right pathway. No hype. No mumbo jumbo. Just the simple truth. Isn't it about time that someone tells you the truth about how to get on the right pathway and stay on it until you have accomplished your lifelong purpose? Of course it is! That is why you will buy this book and read it. You will also buy a few for your family and friends. Why be the only one achieving true happiness? You do want others to succeed. Then, "Pay it Forward". You can, and you will change. You will declare and decree that you will see changes in the lives of those you love by following the simple instructions in this book. There are few guarantees in this life, but I can guarantee this. Everyone is on a pathway. It's time to get on the right one—the Pathway to Christ.

The Pathway to Christ is an essential handbook, a simple step-by-step informational roadmap to help guide you down the pathway of life to arrive safely at your new home. Christianity is about walking and living a life of faith. It is not always easy, and many of the pathways are scary. And the boogieman (Satan) is certainly looking for his next victim, "Be alert, be on watch! Your enemy, the Devil, roams around like a roaring lion, looking for someone to devour" (1 Peter 5:8 Good News T[1]ranslation).

Each section will have a lesson on Biblical principles, fundamentals for living a Christian life, and a better understanding of how to walk in faith. At the end of each lesson, there will be a short quiz to help reinforce what you have read. This will help you build your knowledge of the Word of God. Learning about God and His pathway for us should be fun and enjoyable. It is my endeavor in life to bring back the love of reading and studying the Bible, both individually and as a family. The Bible says, "Study to shew thyself approved unto God, a workman that needeth not to be ashamed, rightly dividing the word of truth"

---

1. https://www.biblegateway.com/passage/?search=1+Peter+5%3A8&version=GNT

(2 Timothy 2:15 K[2]ing James Version). As you learn what God has planned and His purpose for your life, be sure that you stay on the pathway to Christ.

---

2. https://www.biblegateway.com/passage/?search=2+Timothy+2%3A15&version=KJV

In the Beginning

If you confess with your mouth that Jesus is Lord and believe in your heart that God raised him from the dead, you will be saved. 10 For with the heart, one believes and is justified, and with the mouth, one confesses and is saved. (Romans 10:9-10 New International Version)

You can always begin again in life and love, no matter what happens! You can always start with a new beginning. You may fall time and time again. You may even fail a few times, but know this: you can always get up and start again. The wonderful thing about God is that He is a God of second chances. And if you are like me, not perfect by any stretch of the imagination, He is a God of many changes.

Saul to Paul:

The apostle Paul eloquently wrote to the church in Rome, as he had done so often throughout his life as a follower of Christ (something that he could not always brag about). In his writings, he encapsulates the fundamental basics of the Christian conversion, which he knew all too well from his conversion on the road to Damascus (Acts 9[1] New KJV). Paul told those in Rome, "If you confess with your mouth that Jesus is Lord...you will be saved" (Romans 10:9[2] NKJV). This shows that it is an essential act of faith by a new convert (Christian). However, it is necessary to note that one's audible profession of faith does not save you. Salvation only comes by grace through the gift of our faith, not by the words we speak (Ephesians 2:8-9[3] NKJV). Therefore, with all Scripture, if we are to truly and adequately understand it, the context is of critical importance.

Amazingly, when the Book of Romans was authored, typically, the way a person accepted Christ and confessed Him as Lord was through persecution. In many cases, it resulted in their death. It was sure that if you profess Christ and embrace Him, knowing that persecution was sure to follow, it was the work of the Holy Ghost and an indication of true salvation. Therefore, the confession

---

1. https://www.biblegateway.com/passage/?search=Acts+9&version=NKJV

2. https://www.biblegateway.com/passage/?search=Romans+10%3A9&version=NKJV

3. https://www.biblegateway.com/passage/?search=Ephesians+2%3A8-9&version=NKJV

of Christ publicly did not save them. Anyone could shout out loud, "I confess Christ," and not be a Christian, especially from prosecution. However, for those who knew their death was inevitable, it was because of their confession of Christ that they had been saved. Only that type of boldness and faith comes in, knowing they belong to Him. They had to have faith in knowing that if they just called out to Him, they would be saved; maybe not from physical death at that moment, but saved in their hearts spiritually. "Whoever calls on the name of the Lord will be saved" (Romans 10:13[4] NKJV).

Looking at the tenth verse, "for he believes for himself in *his* heart into righteousness and confesses for himself with *his* mouth into salvation." Two key elements here. First, "believe" is vital in the Christian's conversion. Second, "confess" or to "confirm," meaning that you are confirming with your mouth outwardly what has taken place (the change) on the inside (the heart) and are thankful for that change. The word "salvation" or "deliverance" is made accessible from that which binds you. This was evidence of an individual's genuine salvation. If you are genuinely saved (set free), you will confess Christ as Lord and Savior. Because faith has already been instilled in their hearts by Christ Jesus, "Now faith is the assurance (title deed, confirmation) of things hoped for (divinely guaranteed), and the evidence of things not seen, the conviction of their reality—faith comprehends as fact what cannot be experienced by the physical senses" (Hebrews 11:1 Amplified Bible[5]).

Due to his conversion, Saul of Tarsus was the most widely read apostle who followed Jesus. Saul was born to a *Jewish* Family in a city called Tarsus, located in Cilicia, around AD 1-5. At a very young age, Saul received prestigious religious training from one of the best Rabbinical schools in Jerusalem. The school was headed by a well-known Pharisee named Rabban Gamaliel (Rabban means teacher). This teacher was highly respected by all in the religious community. Gamaliel was well respected insomuch that he stood up to intervene on behalf of Jesus when he was arrested and brought before the Sanhedrin courts (Act 5:34-39[6] NKJV); it did not matter how respected

---

4. https://www.biblegateway.com/passage/?search=Romans+10%3A13&version=NKJV

5. https://www.biblegateway.com/passage/?search=Hebrews+11%3A1+&version=AMP

6. https://www.biblegateway.com/passage/?search=Act+5%3A34-39&version=NKJV

Gamaliel was within the counsel, Jesus was still convicted of a crime He did not commit, which was the sin of blasphemy, and crucified on a cross—under Gamaliel's teachings in Tarsus, Saul, later known as Paul, developed his proficient familiarity with the Hebrew Scriptures. His educational and professional credentials permitted him to preach in regional synagogues.

Tarsus was considered a "free city" of Rome. In the Roman Empire, some cities governed themselves by their customs and laws. These cities had the privilege of selecting their magistrates. Being a free city, Tarsus was not subject to having Roman guards stationed at their gates. This fact granted Saul *Roman citizenship*, a privilege he certainly exercised later in his life when deemed necessary (Acts 22:25-28[7] NKJV). Why was having Roman citizenship such a prize to be coveted? Because anyone who possessed such a title enjoyed all the advantages of being a Roman citizen, including special treatment (favors and even protection). The privileges included voting rights in the assembly's legal institutions and eligibility to run for civil or public offices. It also allowed one immunity from certain legal obligations and taxes. So, as you can see, even in the 1st century, there was partiality and favoritism amongst certain ethnic groups, and it was at the expense of the non-citizens. But truth be told, this dichotomy was written about throughout the Bible, and James wrote about it because it was a sin (James 2:1-13[8] NKJV).

Gamaliel greatly influenced Saul's entire life. Personally and Spiritually. Saul often traveled from Tarsus to Rome to meet with other religious leaders. On his way back to Tarsus, Saul heard a lot of commotion from a crowd of people yelling and screaming at a man named Stephen. Saul was thirty years of age (not a very young man), and he witnessed the death of Stephen by stoning (Acts 7:58-58[9] NKJV). This incident took place just a few years after the savage crucifixion of Jesus. It was one of the most shocking displays of Jewish hatred towards Jesus and his followers by the religious authorities that was recorded in the New Testament (Matthew 27:35[10] NKJV). The stoning of Stephen, a

---

7. https://www.biblegateway.com/passage/?search=Acts+22%3A25-28&version=NKJV

8. https://www.biblegateway.com/passage/?search=James+2%3A1-13&version=NKJV

9. https://www.biblegateway.com/passage/?search=Acts+7%3A58-58&version=NKJV

10. https://www.biblegateway.com/passage/?search=Matthew+27%3A35&version=NKJV

follower of Christ Jesus, was the first recorded introduction of Saul in the New Testament.

Stephen the First Martyr:

Stephen was one of the very first deacons (church officials) appointed by the disciples in the early church. A few short years after the death, burial, and resurrection of Christ Jesus, the new believers began to come together and combine all their resources. In Acts 6:1[11] English Standard Version it says, "And in those days as the disciples were increasing in *number* there was a complaint of the Hellenist (according to the One New Man Bible, Hellenists were Jewish Israelis who had adopted the Greek ways), against the Hebrews, because their widows were being neglected in the daily service." The Greeks who were there, amongst the Hebrews, began complaining about how the Hebrew's services were conducted. And the unfair treatment of some of their members. Even in the early church, some complained about things happening in the church's service. Seeing the disarray in the church and how the widows were being mistreated, the disciples called the people together and explained to them that their jobs were not to leave the word of God to wait tables and serve food but to teach and preach (Acts 6:2[12] ESV).

After sharing the importance of their jobs and roles as followers of Christ, the disciples chose seven men: Stephen, a man full of faith and *the* Holy Spirit; Philip, Prochoro, Nicanor, and Timon, and Parmenas, and Nicolas, a proselyte from Antioch (Acts 6:5[13] ESV). These men were of honest report and full of the Holy Spirit, and thus, was the start of the very first official church deacon board (Acts 6:3[14]); these seven men were selected to care for or serve the church ("service" would be the giving of the food, clothing, and other necessities that were provided by the congregation), and for the widows.

Stephen was very zealous and a steadfast defender of Christ and the gospel (Good News); Christianity was called "The Way" in the first few years after the

---

11. https://www.biblegateway.com/passage/?search=Acts+6%3A1+&version=ESV

12. https://www.biblegateway.com/passage/?search=Acts+6%3A2&version=ESV

13. https://www.biblegateway.com/passage/?search=Acts+6%3A5&version=ESV

14. https://www.biblegateway.com/passage/?search=Acts+6%3A3&version=ESV

Holy Spirit came. Stephen's name could imply that he was Greek. He was not a dumb man, as Stephen was well-educated in the history of the Jewish people, a man "full of faith, and the Holy Spirit" (Acts 2:1-4[15] ESV). He preached *Christ and Him crucified* (cf. 1 Corinthians 1:23 NKJV[16]). His message was about Christ's life, death, burial, and resurrection. For this, he was hated and murdered by the same mobs that cried out at Jesus' trials, "Crucify him!" (Matthew 26:23-24[17] ESV). Because Stephen was one that God used in a great way to perform wonders and miracles in Jerusalem (Acts 6:8-14[18] ESV), many Jews in the outer provinces started to question and argue with him. But they could not trip him up because he was full of the Holy Spirit and wisdom (v.9[19]). Just as the people tried to trip up Jesus, and as with Jesus (because they could not outsmart the Holy Spirit), they conspired and lied, convinced others to bear false witness against him (v.10[20]). The people lied and accused Stephen of blasphemy of Moses and God. According to the Judaism customs and law instituted by Moses in the Old Testament, this was a crime punishable by death. It was an act of showing contempt; it was to insult and express a lack of reverence toward God. The person who committed the act of blasphemy was put to death by stoning.

Those who accused, or better yet, those who bore false witness of Stephen, brought up their false claims to the Sanhedrin (vv.11-12[21]). There were smaller Sanhedrin courts with 23 lesser judges in each town. Still, this Sanhedrin was known as the great Sanhedrin court (which meant "council-chamber." 1901. in Smith Bible Dictionary) or supreme council during the times of ancient Israel. The Sanhedrin council comprised 71 of the most religiously educated men in Jerusalem, and the high priest was recognized as the council president. Its members were chief priests or vice chief justices, scribes, and elders. Pharisees and Sadducees were the very wealthy Sadducees who controlled the house,

---

15. https://www.biblegateway.com/passage/?search=ACts+2%3A1-4&version=ESV

16. https://www.biblegateway.com/passage/?search=1+Corinthians+1%3A23&version=NKJV

17. https://www.biblegateway.com/passage/?search=Matthew+26%3A23-24&version=ESV

18. https://www.biblegateway.com/passage/?search=Acts+6%3A8-14&version=ESV

19. https://www.biblegateway.com/passage/?search=Acts+6%3A9&version=ESV

20. https://www.biblegateway.com/passage/?search=Acts+6%3A10&version=ESV

21. https://www.biblegateway.com/passage/?search=Acts+6%3A11-12&version=ESV

much like the US government today. How one was chosen to be a part of the Sanhedrin council is unknown.

The charges of false witness against Stephen claimed that they heard Stephen talking about Jesus, saying that he would destroy the Temple (vv.13-14[22]); this was not the truth of what Jesus said, nor was he talking about a physical Temple. Going back to the day in question, John 2:13-22[23] _ESV,_ there are accounts of Jesus going to Jerusalem for the Passover of the Jewish people. Jesus wanted to be in the city to be present in the Temple. However, when he got there, he noticed the selling of cattle and sheep, doves, and those exchanging money were seated inside the house of God! (v.14[24]) This not only broke his heart, but it inflamed Jesus to the point that he grabbed a whip and started whipping many of the merchants in the Temple (v.15[25]). Jesus yelled, "You must take all this from this place, you must not make My Father's House a house of market" (v.16[26]). Now this, in turn, outraged the religious leaders that were following him. These leaders attempted to find hard evidence on Jesus to bring him up on charges. What gave this man the _right_ to whip these people out of the Temple? His disciples then remembered (v.17[27]) that it is written: "The zeal of Your House will consume Me" (Psalms 69:10 NIV; John 2:17[28]).

The Jewish leaders came to him and said, "What sign do You show us, since You do these things?" (v.18[29]). Jesus answered and said to them, "Destroy this temple, (Sanctuary, literally translating one's body: (cf. 1 Corinthians 6:19[30] NIV; 2 Cor. 6:16[31]) and in three days I shall raise it" (v.19[32]). That was the

---

22. https://www.biblegateway.com/passage/?search=Acts+6%3A13-14&version=ESV

23. https://www.biblegateway.com/passage/?search=John+2%3A13-22+&version=ESV

24. https://www.biblegateway.com/passage/?search=John+2%3A14+&version=ESV

25. https://www.biblegateway.com/passage/?search=John+2%3A15&version=ESV

26. https://www.biblegateway.com/passage/?search=John+2%3A16&version=ESV

27. https://www.biblegateway.com/passage/?search=John+2%3A17&version=ESV

28. https://www.biblegateway.com/passage/?search=Psalm+69%3A9%2CJohn+2%3A17&version=NIV

29. https://www.biblegateway.com/passage/?search=John+2%3A18&version=ESV

30. https://www.biblegateway.com/passage/?search=1+Cor.+6%3A19&version=NIV

31. https://www.biblegateway.com/passage/?search=2+Cor.+6%3A16&version=ESV

32. https://www.biblegateway.com/passage/?search=John+2%3A19&version=ESV

tipping of the religious scale. How would this simple human being destroy a physical structure that took forty-six years to build? (*The temple of Jerusalem, built by Solomon and destroyed by Nebuchadnezzar, took the nation of Israel (led by Zerubbabel) some forty-six years to build. This was the second temple under construction when Jesus was on earth. Bible Odyssey*). And does he expect to raise *it* in three days? (v.20[33]).

Stephen's defense, detailing and outlining the history of the Jews from the time of Abraham through the prophets, was powerful. Insomuch that when he concluded his message, he stated that the Sanhedrin had killed the prophesied Messiah, Jesus of Nazareth. Those in the crowd got furious and enraged with him, "And all that sat in the council, looking steadfastly on him, saw his face as it had been the face of an angel" (Acts 6:15[34] ESV). In Acts chapter 7[35], "When they heard these things, there were cut to the heart, and they gnashed on him their teeth. But he, being full of the Holy Ghost, looked up steadfastly into heaven, and saw the glory of God, and Jesus standing on the right hand of God" (vv.54-55[36]). That mob got even more furious and irritated with Stephen and dragged him out of the city, then stoned him (v.58[37]). This is the moment Saul, aka Paul, comes into our story, bringing us back to where we left off. The people laid their coats at Saul's feet while they picked up several rocks to throw at Stephen.

Saul witnessed the murder of Stephen, and while Stephen was being stoned to death, he called upon God and said as he kneeled to the ground dying, "Lord, do not hold this sin against them." (v.60[38]). After speaking those words, the Bible says, "he fell asleep" and died.

It was not until the Damascus road experience that Saul, now known as Paul, had the pivotal life-changing event (Acts 9:1-22 NKJV[39]); this was the

33. https://www.biblegateway.com/passage/?search=John+2%3A20&version=ESV

34. https://www.biblegateway.com/passage/?search=Acts+6%3A15&version=ESV

35. https://www.biblegateway.com/passage/?search=Acts+7&version=ESV

36. https://www.biblegateway.com/passage/?search=Acts+7%3A54-55&version=KJV

37. https://www.biblegateway.com/passage/?search=Acts+7%3A58&version=KJV

38. https://www.biblegateway.com/passage/?search=Acts+7%3A60&version=NIV

39. https://www.biblegateway.com/passage/?search=Acts+9%3A1-22&version=NKJV

beginning of his new walk in Christ. Saul was on his way to Damascus from Jerusalem after he received official letters from the high priest to round up all those who were now a part of the Christian faith back to Jerusalem to be murdered. While traveling on the road to Damascus one afternoon, Saul was struck blind by an extremely bright light. It was so intense that he was thrown from his horse. While on the ground, he heard a voice, "Saul, Saul, why are you persecuting Me?" (Acts 9:4 NKJV[40]). Saul answered, "Who are You, Lord?" Then the Lord said, "I am Jesus, whom you are persecuting. It is hard for you to kick against the pricks (thorns)" (v.5[41]). Saul, having been struck down blind off his horse, had to be led into the city by his traveling companions he rode with to round up Christians and persecute them, as he is was now unable to see. Such an experience was an event that changed Saul's life forever. He went from an assassin for Rome to an apostle for Christ.

This event led Saul to his total life-altering repentance and receiving the full baptism of the Holy Spirit while under the care of a prophet named Ananias (Acts 9:17-18[42] NIV). Throughout Paul's life, he spent the last thirty-five years sacrificing, suffering, and accomplishing some of the most extraordinary Biblical events known to man at the blessed age of sixty-six. Paul was put to death by beheading with a sword somewhere near Rome between 62 and 67 AD. But like many other Biblical events, we probably never know the accurate dates.

An important note to remember here in your new beginning: public confession, baptism, and all works of good deeds are not the means of salvation but the evidence of salvation!

Essential events in Paul's life: 2 Corinthians 11:21-33[43] NKJV

- The witnessing of Stephen's stoning

---

40. https://www.biblegateway.com/passage/?search=Acts+9%3A4&version=NKJV

41. https://www.biblegateway.com/passage/?search=Acts+9%3A5&version=NKJV

42. https://www.biblegateway.com/passage/?search=Acts+9%3A17-18&version=NIV

43. https://www.biblegateway.com/passage/?search=2+Corinthians+11%3A21-33&version=NKJV

- Received three years of personal teaching Jesus while living in Arabia

- Resurrected at least one person from the dead

- Carried out at least five evangelistic journeys

- Visited more than 50 cities

- Five times received thirty-nine stripes

- Beaten three times with rods

- Stoned once

- Shipwrecked three times

- Was Robbed

- Bitten by a snake

- Left out in the cold, naked, thirsty, and hungry

- Let down a wall in a basket to escape the governor under Aretas, the king

- Preached the gospel to Emperor Caesar and his entire household

- Wrote no less than fourteen books (epistles/letters) of the Bible (no other author can say that)

- Trained and instructed other evangelists and preachers of the gospel (John Mark and Timothy)

- He endured more than five years in prison

In the Beginning: Quiz

1. Who was the author of the Book of Romans?

2. This is an essential act of faith on the part of a new convert (Christian):

3. Salvation only comes by __________, through the__________ of our __________, not by the words we __________ (Ephesians 2:8-9[1]):

4. What occurs when someone calls on the name of the Lord?

5. What does Romans 10:9-10[2] say?

6. In your own words, explain what Romans 10:9-10[3] means to you:

7. Who is the Author of the Book of Acts?

8. What was the name of the city where Saul was born?

9. Where was Saul going when he was knocked from his horse and blinded, and why?

10. Name three events in Paul's life:

---

1. https://www.biblegateway.com/passage/?search=Ephesians+2%3A8-9&version=NIV

2. https://www.biblegateway.com/passage/?search=Romans+10%3A9-10+&version=NIV

3. https://www.biblegateway.com/passage/?search=Romans+10%3A9-10+&version=NIV

Notes to Self:

In the Middle

Count it all joy, my brothers, when you meet trials of various kinds, 3 for you know that the testing of your faith produces steadfastness. 4 And let steadfastness have its full effect,

that you may be perfect and complete, lacking in nothing.

(James 1:2-4 New International Version)

Three essential factors on how to live life during trouble and still have joy: James and Peter.

1. The Joy the World Gives Is Not the Same Joy That God Gives:

Accepting Christ into your heart and beginning your new life in Him does not mean that all your troubles will magically disappear. In fact, at times, they may seem to be amplified. If you had bills before you got saved, guess what? You are still going to have those identical bills. If you had problems on your job or in your relationship before Christ, sorry to say, those same issues and concerns will still be there after receiving Christ. However, (and here's the good news), being that you now have a love of Christ and the Holy Spirit dwelling inside you, many of those same issues and problems you had or have will be faced with a new attitude. Instead of cursing, fussing, fighting, and running away from the problems, you can turn them over to Christ to help you face them with His help.

James:

In James' writing to the church, he encouraged and instructed them to have faith in their trials so that their faith could develop perseverance. The problem that seems to arise with many new believers is that when trouble and tough times come continuously upon them, they begin to question their faith, and two they want to know "why?". How could they experience so much hardship and still have joy? Being *in the middle of* a crisis is the last place to think of counting anything joyful. Romans 15:13[1] NIV says, "May the God of hope fill

---

1. https://www.biblegateway.com/passage/?search=Romans+15%3A13+&version=NIV

you with all joy and peace as your trust in him, so that you may overflow with hope by the power of the Holy Spirit."

I. Peter: Five things he was known for.

1. Peter was one of Jesus' disciples (Matthew 4:18[2] <u>NIV</u>);

2. Peter, the one called the "Rock" (Matthew 16:18[3] <u>NIV</u>). 3. The same Peter that walked on water (Matthew 14:28[4]). 4. He is the same Peter that cut off a man's ear in the Garden of Gethsemane (Matthew 26:51[5]) 5. And the same Peter who denied Christ three times (Matthew 26:69-75[6]). He also dealt with joy in the middle of trials, "In this, you greatly rejoice, though now for a little while, you may have to suffer grief in all kinds of trials. 7 These have come so that the proven genuineness of your faith—of greater worth than gold, which perishes even though refined by fire—may result in praise, glory, and honor when Jesus Christ is revealed. 8 Though you have not seen him, you love him; even though you do not see him now, you believe in him and filled with an inexpressible and glorious joy. 9 For you are receiving the end result of your faith, the salvation of your souls." (1 Peter 1:6-9[7] <u>NIV</u>).

Both James and Peter's passages instruct us on what we should do in the middle of stress, worry, trials, and hardships. James said, "Consider it pure joy..." and Peter said, "In this you greatly rejoice..." Why? Well, one good reason is that our trials make us stronger. James's letter to the church stated, "Faith develops perseverance" when keeping faith through trials. How does this happen? By the testing of our faith, that's how. Peter reassures that "our faith, which is priceless, will be proved genuine and result in praise to God" (1 Peter 1:7 NIV[8]). Joy is mentioned second of the fruit of the Spirit; it is plentiful; like a bottomless well of water, there is always an abundance of joy. Even in your darkest nights, when

---

2. https://www.biblegateway.com/passage/?search=Matthew+4%3A18&version=NIV

3. https://www.biblegateway.com/passage/?search=Matthew+16%3A18&version=NIV

4. https://www.biblegateway.com/passage/?search=Matthew+14%3A28&version=NIV

5. https://www.biblegateway.com/passage/?search=Matthew+26%3A51&version=NIV

6. https://www.biblegateway.com/passage/?search=Matthew+26%3A69-75&version=NIV

7. https://www.biblegateway.com/passage/?search=1+Peter+1%3A6-9&version=NIV

8. https://www.biblegateway.com/passage/?search=1+Peter+1%3A7&version=NIV

grief from loss seems to overtake you, sadness may overwhelm you but know that God's joy is there in the middle of it with you.

II. God's Joy Cannot Be Taken Away:

There will come times when all hell is breaking loose, and everything around you is in chaos; it seems like all hope is lost! But it's not. As a believer, the Holy Spirit promises you that you will have His constant presence with you, a promise even in ancient times, "Be strong and courageous. Do not be afraid or terrified because of them, for the Lord your God goes with you; he will never leave you nor forsake you" (Deuteronomy 31:6 NKJV[9]). We are promised His joy, and God says that the joy of the Lord is your strength, "The Lord is my strength and my shield; my heart trusts in him, and he helps me. My heart leaps for joy, and with my song, I praise him" (Psalms 28:7 NKJV[10]); this is assured, just like our salvation, through the one-time sacrifice of Christ Jesus. John wrote about the joy of the Lord being in us and that it may be complete, "These things have I spoken unto you, that my joy might remain in you, and that your joy might be full (complete)" (John 15:11 KJV[11]).

At other times in the Bible, the disciples are filled with joy. Acts 13:52[12] NKJV says, "And the disciples were filled with joy and the Holy Spirit." And the jailer that was in charge of Paul and Silas (Act 16:23-24[13]) was filled with much joy, as was his entire house, "And when he had brought them into his house, he set a meal before them; and rejoiced [he was filled with joy], because he had come to believe in God with his whole house" (Acts 16:34[14]).

True joy comes in your walk of faith, which can bring trials, tribulations, and much satisfaction. It takes great faith to live a life one does not understand entirely. "How do you truly trust someone you have never met or seen?" is a worldwide question that thousands have wondered about. To have this type

---

9. https://www.biblegateway.com/passage/?search=Deuteronomy+31%3A6&version=NKJV

10. https://www.biblegateway.com/passage/?search=Psalms+28%3A7&version=NKJV

11. https://www.biblegateway.com/passage/?search=John+15%3A11+&version=KJV

12. https://www.biblegateway.com/passage/?search=Acts+13%3A52+&version=NKJV

13. https://www.biblegateway.com/passage/?search=Act+16%3A23-24&version=NKJV

14. https://www.biblegateway.com/passage/?search=Act+16%3A34&version=NKJV

of faith, you must truly understand who God is and how He is revealed throughout the Bible. Having and knowing about this kind of faith will be discussed later in this course. But be assured that no one can take God's joy away. That's genuine faith.

III. You Have to Grab onto God's Joy:

Stop whining and complaining! Joy is free, just like salvation. It's a gift and one that is perfect, given by God. Therefore, we must reach out and accept God's gift to us. Grab onto it and hold it tight, like it's a lifeline. Your life depends on it! Your happiness relies on it. Your health needs it. Make a conscious, deliberate decision to have joy daily over anger, bitterness, and sorrow, no matter what.

Look at the following Bible examples of how believers faced severe trials and extreme poverty. Their overflowing joy welled up in generosity that was great in richness (2 Corinthians 8:2-3[15] NKJV). Despite severe suffering, they welcomed the message of Christ with joy by the Holy Spirit (1 Thessalonians 1:6[16] NKJV). Even when all hope seemed lost, they were encouraged to "Be joyful always" (1 Thessalonians 5:16[17] NJKV). They lost property, but they were still joyful and sympathized with those who were cast into prison because of their faith. It didn't faze them because they knew they had better and lasting possessions in heaven (Hebrews 10:34[18] NKJV). The best example of them all is in Hebrews 12:2[19], "Let us fix our eyes on Jesus, the author and perfecter of our faith, who for the joy set before him endured the cross, scorning its shame, and sat down at the right hand of the throne of God."

The Bible shows the church persecuted and endured many trials, tribulations, and hardships. And just like those who were new in their faith, we must learn how to face our difficulties and grab onto God's joy while in the middle of severe persecution or even death. No matter what, choose joy. You will have

---

15. https://www.biblegateway.com/passage/?search=2+Corinthians+8%3A2-3&version=NKJV

16. https://www.biblegateway.com/passage/?search=1+Thessalonians+1%3A6&version=NKJV

17. https://www.biblegateway.com/passage/?search=1+Thessalonians+5%3A16&version=NIV

18. https://www.biblegateway.com/passage/?search=Hebrews+10%3A34&version=NKJV

19. https://www.biblegateway.com/passage/?search=Hebrews+12%3A2&version=NKJV

to face all types of overwhelming odds, sickness, disappointments, heartaches, monthly bills, insurmountable obstacles, and many even divorce, bankruptcy, and foreclosure. It doesn't sound pleasant, but you must know this is life. However, you will discover that in the middle of all hell breaking loose, God's joy is true and there with you. You will find joy in each trial, and you can rejoice greatly with inexpressible joy, full of glory. You can endure whatever comes your way because if you have been saved through faith in Christ Jesus, you have all you need. So, grab onto God's joy and hold on tight. "For his anger lasts only a moment, but his favor lasts a lifetime! Weeping may last through the night, but joy comes with the morning" (Psalm 30:5 NLT[20]). Let me encourage you with this: IT'S MORNING TIME! Finding Joy in the Middle of It All That's Wisdom.

---

20. https://www.biblegateway.com/passage/?search=Psalm+30%3A5+&version=NLT

In the Middle: Quiz

1. What are the three essential factors for living life amid trouble and still having joy?

a.

b.

c.

2. Does accepting Christ in your heart mean all problems will cease? Why or why not?

3. Why did James write to the church?

4. Peter was known for:

a.

b.

c.

d.

5. What does Deuteronomy 31:6[1] say?

6. True joy comes in your _______________ walk.

7. The _________ of the __________ is your ____________ (Nehemiah 8:10[2]).

8. No matter what, choose ________.

9. Throughout the Bible, we see the church being ________________.

10. What should you do with God's joy?

---

1. https://www.biblegateway.com/passage/?search=Deuteronomy+31%3A6+&version=NKJV

2. https://www.biblegateway.com/passage/?search=Neh.+8%3A10&version=NKJV

Notes to Self:

What Faith, Now Faith

Now, faith is confidence in what we hope for and assurance about what we do not see.

(Hebrews 11:1 NIV)

One of the most essential elements in a person's life is faith. You must believe it! Whether you are a Christian or non-Christian, faith is the fundamental foundation of everyday life. People worldwide demonstrate faith every minute of the day, knowingly and unknowingly. Hebrews 11:1[1] NKJV is the true definition of what faith is. It is trusting in something you explicitly cannot prove. What we believe is based on what we have heard, what we hear, what was or is said to or around us, and what we are conditioned (programmed) into us by our teachers, parents, siblings, friends, and society when we are children.

There are two aspects of faith: One is Intellectual assent, and the other is Trust. The first aspect, Intellectual assent, is believing something to be true. Is it true just because you think it? Does that make it accurate? Just because I say, "The sky is green, and my grass is blue," does not make it accurate. The evidence of truth is looking at the sky and grass and *seeing* that it is wrong. The sky is blue, and the grass is green. So, what I chose to believe to be true was not true at all. How do we deal with that? For years, we have been told and taught things all our lives. Things that others claim to be true. But as we all grow up and learn what is and what isn't genuine or correct, we still have a choice to believe it or not. It is called our belief system. We have a choice to continue to believe in it or not. But for someone to continue to believe in something incorrect is beyond me.

Trust is the second aspect of faith. Trust is relying on facts that something is true. A Chair is the best example for illustrating these two aspects. Intellectual assent is recognizing the chair and agreeing that it is designed to support and hold up a person when they sit on it. Trust is physically sitting on the chair. Okay, we believe that it is a chair, and we believe that it was designed to support and hold a person. But we still must physically sit in the chair. Similarly, we must entirely and personally rely on the death of Jesus as the only atoning

---

1. https://www.biblegateway.com/passage/?search=Hebrews+11%3A1&version=NKJV

sacrifice for our sins, "But God demonstrates his love for us in this: While we were still sinners, Christ died for us" (Romans 5:8[2] NIV).

It is crucial to understand these two aspects of faith. When it comes to Jesus, many people believe specific facts about him. Many will intellectually agree with the Bible regarding the facts about Jesus. However, knowing those facts to be true is not what "faith" means in the Bible. The definition of faith, biblically, requires intellectual assent to the facts and trust in the facts.

Saying you believe in something is a straightforward thing to do. However, it is not enough to believe that Jesus is God incarnated, died on the cross, buried in a grave, and then resurrected on the third day to pay the penalty for our sins. Because the Bible says that even the demons *believe* in God, and they also acknowledge those facts, "You believe that there is one God. Good! Even the demons believe that—and shudder!" (James 2:19 ESV[3]). The Bible is clear when it says that faith is the belief one has in the one true God without seeing Him.

Where does this type of faith come from? It's certainly not something we dream up all on our own. And it is not something that we are born with. And as much as I enjoy studying and pursuing knowledge, it is not a result of all our diligence in researching and pursuing spiritual things. Faith is indeed a gift that comes from God Himself. A gift that no one can work for. "For by *grace* you have been saved through faith. And this is not your own doing; it is the gift of God, not a result of works, as that no one may boast" (Ephesians 2:8-9[4] ESV). Faith is given by God, along with His mercy and grace, according to His perfect will, plan, and purpose for our lives. And He gets all the glory for it.

We must demonstrate our faith and trust in God because, according to the Bible, our faith is essential to Christianity. Without faith, it is impossible to please Him (Heb. 11:6[5] ESV), and without trust in Him, we have no place in Him. Therefore, in his letter, James encouraged the church to consider when

---

2. https://www.biblegateway.com/passage/?search=Romans+5%3A8&version=NIV

3. https://www.biblegateway.com/passage/?search=James+2%3A19+&version=ESV

4. https://www.biblegateway.com/passage/?search=Ephesians+2%3A8-9&version=ESV

5. https://www.biblegateway.com/passage/?search=Heb.+11%3A6&version=ESV

we fall into trials. It is *pure joy* because when we are tested in our faith, it produces perseverance, and over time, it will mature us by strengthening our walk, proving that our faith is genuine. "Count it all joy, my brothers, when you meet trials of various kinds, 3 for you know that the testing of your faith produces steadfastness. 4 And let steadfastness have its full effect, that you may be perfect and complete, lacking in nothing" (James 1:2-4[6] ESV).

The question is, "What increases our faith?". The answer is to draw *closer to God through praying and studying His Word.* That seems simple, but many people don't like to pray and study the word of God. To have a strong relationship with God built on faith, we need to pray (daily) and read His word (daily). We are inundated daily with worry and stress, not knowing how to make ends meet when the ends never meet.

In his letter to the Philippians, Paul encouraged them, "Do not be anxious about anything [don't worry or stress], but in every situation, by prayer and petition, with thanksgiving, present your requests to God. 7 And the peace of God, which transcends all understanding, will guard your hearts and your minds in Christ Jesus" (Philippians 4:6-7[7] ESV).

Three ways how we grow in faith:

1. By confessing our sins (John 1:7[8] NKJV; 1 John 1:9[9])
2. By seeking Him (Ps. 27:8[10] NKJV; Isa. 55:6[11])
3. By Surrendering to Him (Gal. 3:3[12] NKJV; Col 2:6[13]; Rom. 12:1[14])

---

6. https://www.biblegateway.com/passage/?search=James+1%3A2-4&version=ESV

7. https://www.biblegateway.com/passage/?search=Philippians+4%3A6-7&version=ESV

8. https://www.biblegateway.com/passage/?search=John+1%3A7&version=NKJV

9. https://www.biblegateway.com/passage/?search=1+John+1%3A9&version=NKJV

10. https://www.biblegateway.com/passage/?search=Ps.+27%3A8&version=NKJV

11. https://www.biblegateway.com/passage/?search=Isa.+55%3A6&version=NKJV

12. https://www.biblegateway.com/passage/?search=Gal.+3%3A3&version=NKJV

13. https://www.biblegateway.com/passage/?search=Col+2%3A6&version=NKJV

14. https://www.biblegateway.com/passage/?search=Rom.+12%3A1&version=NKJV

What Faith, Now Faith: Quiz

1. What is one of the most important elements in a person's life?

2. What are the two aspects of faith?

a.

b.

3. What does the Bible say about the demons believing in James 2:19[1]?

4. This is what we believe is based on:

5. What is faith? (Eph.2:8-9[2]):

6. Without it, it is impossible to please God _______________.

7. James tells us to consider our fall into trials as what?

8. How is our faith increased?

9. In Philippians 4:6-7[3] Paul encourages the church to _________________.

10. What are the three ways we grow in our faith? (Include scripture ref.)

Notes to Self:

---

1. https://www.biblegateway.com/passage/?search=James+2%3A19&version=NKJV

2. https://www.biblegateway.com/passage/?search=Eph.2%3A8-9&version=NKJV

3. https://www.biblegateway.com/passage/?search=Philippians+4%3A6-7+&version=NKJV

New Creation

Therefore, if anyone is in Christ, he is a new creation; old things have passed away;

behold, all things have become new.

(2 Corinthians 5:17 NKJV)

Everyone loves a new beginning. We want to be able to start all over again, fresh and new. Whether it's a new job, getting a new car or house, or maybe even starting over in a new relationship. We all like the feeling that comes with something new.

One of the best-known spiritual ways for man to start over is by giving their life to Christ. As Paul stated in 2 Corinthians 5:17[1] NKJV, one of the most quoted scriptures to date, "Therefore, if anyone *is* in Christ, *he is* a new creation; old things have passed away; behold, all things have become new." What is interesting is the word "therefore"; if we look at the previous verses here, in verses 14-16[2], Paul writes that all believers have died with Christ and no longer live for themselves. We are now spiritual and no longer live for the world. Our old sinful nature was nailed to the cross with Jesus. It was crucified, died, and buried with Him. And when the Father raised Him, we too were raised to *walk in the newness of life,* 'Therefore we were buried with Him through baptism into death, that just as Christ was raised from the dead by the glory of the Father, even so we also should walk in newness of life" (Romans 6:4 NKJV[3]).

Here is what we need to understand and grasp about the new creation: it is just that, a creation. It is something that God, the Father and Creator of all, created. This new birth that the will of God brought about each of us experience, as John tells us in John 1:13[4] NKJV, is not inherited, nor do we get to decide to recreate ourselves anew. Let's be clear: God did not simply clean up our old nature. He could have, but when have we read that God takes the easy way out without teaching us a valuable lesson? What God did do was create something

1. https://www.biblegateway.com/passage/?search=2+Corinthians+5%3A17+&version=NKJV

2. https://www.biblegateway.com/passage/?search=2+Corinthians+5%3A14-16&version=NKJV

3. https://www.biblegateway.com/passage/?search=Romans+6%3A4+&version=NKJV

4. https://www.biblegateway.com/passage/?search=John+1%3A13&version=NKJV

unique and fresh. He created something from nothing, completely new, just as He did in making the whole universe. Only God, the true Creator, could accomplish such a feat. No other known or unknown "god" can take credit for that.

The second part of 2 Corinthians 5:17[5] NKJV, "old things have passed away." What is this telling us here? The "old" refers to everything considered part of our old nature. What are some of the old natures? Lovers of sin, natural pride, passions and bad habits, bad attitudes, unnatural affections, and reliance on works. So, with the passing away, what we once loved has passed away, especially our self-righteousness and self-justification. With the passing away, *the newness has come!* The wonderful part of this is starting over, fresh and new. The new things (life) replace the old stuff (dead).

Many things we did before Christ are no longer something we want to do after accepting Christ. However, you must know this change may not be immediate, so don't beat yourself up if you trip, stumble, and fall. It happens to the best of us. The one thing to remember is not to allow yourself to be tricked into thinking that you cannot continue to live a free life if you trip, stumble, and fall. Ask God to forgive you and get back on track. Self-pity is a tool the enemy uses against us to make us feel sorry for ourselves. You are redeemed and are being sanctified every single day. What does this mean? It means that you are being made holy each day. The desire to sin becomes less and less. As you mature, sinning will become less frequent, even though you will still sin. The apostle Paul knew all too well about our sinful flesh and how it must die daily as we grow in Christ. He exclaims, "I die daily" (1 Corinthians 15:31[6] NKJV). We, too, must die to our flesh daily.

You must know there is a difference between living in sin and continuing to sin. You may ask, "What about those Christians who continue to sin?". Let me share that sinless perfection will never be reached in this life! I have a secret for you: no one is perfect. Surprise! So, consider this before you go ahead and tell that person at your job that they aren't perfect! The Bible says, "Let the redeemed of the Lord say so" (Psalms 107:2[7] NKJV). You have been redeemed, and you

---

5. https://www.biblegateway.com/passage/?search=2+Corinthians+5%3A17&version=NKJV

6. https://www.biblegateway.com/passage/?search=1+Corinthians+15%3A31&version=NKJV

should not keep it to yourself. Share with others what God has done for you, that you are a new creation. God has wiped your slate clean, allowing you to start all over again, fresh and new.

Here is the difference. When you are a new creation, you are no longer a slave to sin as you used to be. You have now been freed from sin, and that sin no longer has power over you, "We know that our old self was crucified with him so that the body of sin might be brought to nothing so that we would no longer be enslaved to sin. 7 For one who has died has been set free from sin" (Romans 6:6-7 ESV[8]). It's now your choice to count yourself "dead to sin but alive to God in Christ Jesus" or "let sin reign" (Romans 6:11-12[9]). You have the power now to choose to be alive to God in Christ Jesus.

As a new Christian, a new creation, what does it mean? It means that you are a person professing belief in Jesus as the Christ (Messiah) or believing in a religion based on the teachings of Jesus as the Christ. However, the dictionary's definition falls short of honestly communicating the biblical meaning of a Christian. As a new creation, you meet the Bible's definition of a Christian.

---

7. https://www.biblegateway.com/passage/?search=Psalms+107%3A2&version=NKJV

8. https://www.biblegateway.com/passage/?search=Romans+6%3A6-7+&version=ESV

9. https://www.biblegateway.com/passage/?search=Romans+6%3A11-12&version=ESV

New Creation: Quiz

1. What does 2 Corinthians 5:17[1] say?

2. If you are a Christian, do you remember, and what was the date you became a new creation?

3. Our old sinful ______________ was ______________ to the ______________ with ______________.

4. What are some of the old natures?

a.

b.

c.

5. The Old things represents ______________________, and the New things represents ______________________.

6. Where is the scripture "I die daily" found?

7. In your own words, what does it mean "Let the redeemed of the Lord say so?"

8. We have been given a choice to be free or enslaved by sin (True or False).

9. We have no power to choose to be alive to God in Christ Jesus (True or False).

10. Everyone loves a new ______________________.

---

1. https://www.biblegateway.com/passage/?search=2+Corinthians+5%3A17+&version=ESV

Notes to Self:

Be the Church

He said to them, "But who do you say that I am?" Simon Peter answered and said, "You are the Christ, the Son of the living God." Jesus answered and said to him, "Blessed are you, Simon Bar-Jonah, for flesh and blood has not revealed this to you, but My Father who is in heaven. And I also say you that you are Peter, and on this rock, I will build my church, and the gates of Hell shall not prevail against it. And I will give you the keys of the kingdom of heaven, and whatever you bind on earth will be bound in heaven,

and whatever you loose on earth will be loosed in heaven.

(Matthew 16:15-19 English Standard Version)

Being the church, what does it mean to be the church of Christ? Not in a denominational meaning but in more of a "spiritual relationship to Christ" meaning. The day the church came alive was on the Day of Pentecost in Acts chapter 2:1-3[1] NKJV: "And when the day of Pentecost was now come, they were all together in one place. 2 And suddenly there came from heaven a sound as of the rushing of a mighty wind, and it filled all the house where they were sitting. 3 And there appeared unto them tongues parting asunder, like as of fire; and it sat upon each one of them". This was the beginning of the first church, or the actual starting of what we call the first church. Keep in mind, the Roman Catholic church was NOT and is NOT the "first church" as many of the Catholic faith may believe.

There is no record anywhere in the New Testament showing where the following acts were performed by the "first church": submitting to a pope, baptizing infants, praying to Mary, observing the ordinances of baptism and the Lord's Supper as sacraments, having a select priesthood, venerating (a ritual act of devotion to) Mary, passing on apostolic authority to successors of the apostles, or praying to saints. These are Roman Catholic core elements of faith and were not practiced by the New Testament Church. Clearly, the study will show that the two are not the same.

The only true and first church that we are to emulate, follow, and model ourselves after is recorded in the New Testament (Acts 2^2). As the Holy Spirit

---

1. https://www.biblegateway.com/passage/?search=Acts+2%3A1-3&version=NKJV

fell upon those in the upper room (Acts 2[3]), this was a miraculous spreading of the Good News of Jesus Christ. It had been ten days since Jesus ascended into heaven, Acts 1:9[4] NKJV: "And when he had said these things, as they were looking on, he was lifted, and a cloud took him out of their sight." The disciples were instructed to go back and wait and pray for the outpouring (indwelling) of the Holy Spirit. There were about 120 people, along with Jesus' disciples, in the upper room, an area above the living quarters used for hosting dinners and parties, and there was no mention of whose house it belonged to. "When the day of Pentecost arrived, they were all together in one place. 2 And suddenly there came from heaven a sound likea mighty rushing wind, and it filled the entire house where they were sitting. 3 And divided tongues as fire appeared to them and rested on each one. 4 And they were all filled with the Holy Spirit and began to speak in other tongues as the Spirit gave them utterance" Acts 2:1-4[5] NKJV.

When Jesus told Peter, "I will build my church," it foretells what would happen once He sent the Holy Spirit back to earth to those who received Him. "But when the Helper comes, whom I will send to you from the Father, the Spirit of truth, who proceeds from the Father, he will bear witness about me. 27 And you also will bear witness, because you have been with me from the beginning" John 15:26-27[6] NKJV; "When the Spirit of truth comes, he will guide you into all the truth, for he will not speak on his authority, but whatever he hears he will speak, and he will declare to you the things that are to come" John 16:13[7].

Many people who are a part of a denominational organization believe that the church is the physical building in which they assemble. They could not be more wrong. The physical structure is not a biblical understanding of the true meaning of the word church. In Greek, ekklesia is translated as "an assembly" or "called out from the world for God." Thayer and Smith. (1999). "Greek

---

2. https://www.biblegateway.com/passage/?search=Acts+2&version=NKJV

3. https://www.biblegateway.com/passage/?search=Acts+2&version=NKJV

4. https://www.biblegateway.com/passage/?search=Acts+1%3A9+&version=NKJV

5. https://www.biblegateway.com/passage/?search=Acts+2%3A1-4+&version=NKJV

6. https://www.biblegateway.com/passage/?search=John+15%3A26-27++&version=NKJV

7. https://www.biblegateway.com/passage/?search=John+16%3A13&version=NKJV

Lexicon entry for Ekklesia". "The NAS New Testament Greek Lexicon[8]". The root meaning is not that of a physical building; it is a body of believers and people. In the book of Romans, Paul refers to the church in their *house*, "Greet the church that is in their house" (Romans 16:5 ESV[9]), not a church building. It was those that came and assembled in one place. The church, the people, are the body of Christ, the church He is the head of, "And God placed all things under his feet and appointed him to be over everything for the church, which is his body, the fullness of him who fills everything in every way" (Ephesians 1:22-23[10] NKJV). So, when you hear "The body of Christ," it is not a denomination, as many may believe; it is made up of all those who are believers in Christ Jesus from the day of Pentecost (Acts 2[11]) and all those who have received Him today, until the day Christ returns.

What would your answer be if someone asked you what church you attend? Like most people, your answer would likely be that of a physical nature, identifying a building. But look at it differently; look at it as you are the physical building (church) in which the Holy Spirit dwells. Just as when Jesus entered the world, there was a physical body prepared for Him (Hebrews 10:5[12] NKJV), and through that body (Philippians 2:7[13] NKJV), He demonstrated the love of God, especially by His death on the cross which was a sacrificial type of love, it was clearly tangible and boldly done, "but God shows his love for us in that while we were still sinners, Christ died for us" Romans 5:8[14] NKJV. You can show this tangible and bold love by sacrificially giving your all to and for Christ. You can be the *real church*.

---

8. http://www.biblestudytools.com/lexicons/greek/nas/

9. https://www.biblegateway.com/passage/?search=Romans+16%3A5&version=NKJV

10. https://www.biblegateway.com/passage/?search=Ephesians+1%3A22-23&version=NKJV

11. https://www.biblegateway.com/passage/?search=Acts+2&version=NKJV

12. https://www.biblegateway.com/passage/?search=Hebrews+10%3A5&version=NKJV

13. https://www.biblegateway.com/passage/?search=Philippians+2%3A7&version=NKJV

14. https://www.biblegateway.com/passage/?search=Romans+5%3A8&version=NKJV

Be the Church: Quiz

1. Who did Jesus say, "Upon this rock, I will build my church" to?

2. Where is the Day of Pentecost found in the Bible?

3. What does *ekklesia* mean?

4. The "Body of Christ" is a denomination (True or

False).

5. You must be in a physical building to be a part of the "body of Christ" (True or False).

6. Is the Roman Catholic church recorded as the first church in the New Testament? (True or False).

7. The "body of Christ" believe and follow Christ (True or False).

8. How many were said to be in the Upper Room?

9. How can you show the love of Christ?

10. What church do you attend?

Notes to Self:

The Holy Spirit

But you shall receive power when the Holy Spirit has come upon you, and you shall be witnesses to Me in Jerusalem, and in all Judea and Samaria, and to the end of the earth.

(Acts 1:8 NKJV)

Growing up in church, I always heard people talking and teaching about the Holy Ghost. But as I got older, I heard more contemporary churches use the term Holy Spirit. Why the change? Some nontraditional churches had the nerve to say that the term Holy Ghost was too spooky, so they started using the term Holy Spirit to draw more people. Seriously?

So, what is the difference between the Holy Ghost and the Holy Spirit? Over the years (and we are talking several hundred years), "Ghost" and "Spirit" have changed places. The King James Version is the only version that uses the "Holy Ghost" of the modern English translations of the Bible that uses the "Holy Ghost" today. If you look up and count how often King James uses the "Holy Ghost," you will see that it occurs 90 times, and the "Holy Spirit" appears seven times. There isn't an apparent reason why those who translated the Bible used Ghost more often than Spirit. In most instances, in some of the recent translations of Scripture, the word "Spirit" replaces "Ghost" (cf. Matthew 28:19; Acts 5:3-4; Acts 28:25-26; 1 Corinthians 12:4-6). No matter what term people use, the Holy Ghost is the active breath of God, blowing where He desires.

What does it mean to be Filled? The Bible says, "And I will pray the Father, and He will give you another Helper, that He may abide with you forever" (John 14:16 NKJV)[1]. Before Jesus left the disciples and ascended into heaven, he promised to send back a "helper" or "comforter" to dwell in all believers. The indwelling of the Holy Spirit is essential to the lives of believers. It is a gift that takes place at the time of believing. Consider it a down payment for future glorification in Jesus Christ, "who also has sealed us and given us the Spirit in our hearts as a guarantee" (2 Corinthians 1:22 NKJV[2]). "And do not grieve

---

1. https://www.biblegateway.com/passage/?search=John+14%3A16+&version=NKJV

2. https://www.biblegateway.com/passage/?search=2+Corinthians+1%3A22+&version=NKJV

the Holy Spirit of God, by whom you were sealed for the day of redemption" (Ephesians 4:30 NKJV[3]).

When we hear and talk about the Holy Spirit, our attention is drawn to chapter 2 of the Book of Acts (also known as the Book of the Holy Spirit) on the Day of Pentecost, after the resurrection of Christ. But that is not the first time we hear of the Holy Spirit appearing to man. We read in the Gospel of Luke 1-2[4] NKJV that before the birth of Jesus, it was John the Baptist (Jesus' first cousin) who was filled with the Holy while still in his mother Elizabeth's womb, "For indeed, as soon as the voice of your greeting sounded in my ears, the babe leaped in my womb for joy" (Luke 1:44 NKJV[5]).

Being filled with the Holy Spirit/Ghost, however, one wants to say both refer to the Third Person of the Holy Trinity. Ah, yes, the Trinity! To understand the Holy Spirit, one must know who the Holy Spirit is and what a significant role He plays in the life of a Christian.

The Bible is clear when it says there is only God (Deut. 6:4[6] NKJV; 1 Cor. 8:4[7]; Gal. 3:20[8]; 1 Tim. 2:5[9]); however, as we study more profound the word, we see that God is three separate and distinct individuals. The Trinity is one of the greatest mysteries known to man. How can one be three? How can there be the same? The simplest way to explain this phenomenon (and in a way that even a child could grasp and visualize its elementary meaning) is by using a subject usually not the favorite in school: chemistry. In this example, one can't help but enjoy its simple lesson. The nature of water (H_20) is one compound that can exist in three separate states: ice, liquid, and vapor. But they are all made of the two natural elements that form water. About our God, this is not the complete picture and does not invalidate His oneness, and it's just a simple way to illustrate His three "persons." The Holy Spirit is an attribute of God.

3. https://www.biblegateway.com/passage/?search=Ephesians+4%3A30++&version=NKJV

4. https://www.biblegateway.com/passage/?search=Luke+1-2++&version=NKJV

5. https://www.biblegateway.com/passage/?search=Luke+1%3A44&version=NKJV

6. https://www.biblegateway.com/passage/?search=Deut.+6%3A4&version=NKJV

7. https://www.biblegateway.com/passage/?search=1+Cor.+8%3A4&version=NKJV

8. https://www.biblegateway.com/passage/?search=Gal.+3%3A20&version=NKJV

9. https://www.biblegateway.com/passage/?search=1+Tim.+2%3A5&version=NKJV

God the Father, God the Son, and God the Holy Spirit. It is a unified Godhead known as the "Trinity" in Christianity. There is no earthly way for man to comprehend and explain this mystery and the complexity of an infinite God. Our little, finite minds cannot explain the heavenly because our minds are earthly. All we do and see regarding the divine is based on our faith, even though we cannot understand why and how certain things are. Our faith is what we stand on in a faithless world (Hebrews 11:1, 3, 6[10] NKJV; 1 Corinthians 2:5-10, 14; 13:12[11]).

We received God and the gift of His Spirit by faith (John 7:37-39[12] NKJV). The moment you receive Christ into your heart is the exact moment the spirit of God dwells within you. "In him you also, when you heard the word of truth, the gospel of your salvation, and believed in him, were sealed with the promised Holy Spirit" Ephesians 1:13[13] NKJV. In the following chapter, we will discuss the Tongues and how they play an essential role in the lives of those saved and filled with the spirit of God (Acts 2:4[14]).

The only way that man can know the things of God is if the Holy Spirit reveals them. The Holy Spirit is intelligent, He has emotions, and He has a will, "For who knows a person's thoughts except the spirit of that person, which is in him? So also no one comprehends the thoughts of God except the Spirit of God" (1 Corinthians 2:11 NKJV[15]). The Holy Spirit has specific functions and roles in our lives for God, "When the Spirit of truth comes, he will guide you into all the truth, for he will not speak on his authority, but whatever he hears he will speak, and he will declare to you the things that are to come" (John 16:13 NKJV[16]). The one thing we will never have to worry about regarding the Holy Spirit is having the right things to say at the right time. The Holy Spirit gives us

---

10. https://www.biblegateway.com/passage/?search=Hebrews+11%3A1%2C+3%2C+6&version=NKJV

11. https://www.biblegateway.com/

    passage/?search=1+Corinthians+2%3A5-10%2C+14%3B+13%3A12&version=NKJV

12. https://www.biblegateway.com/passage/?search=John+7%3A37-39&version=NKJV

13. https://www.biblegateway.com/passage/?search=Ephesians+1%3A13+&version=NKJV

14. https://www.biblegateway.com/passage/?search=Acts+2%3A4&version=NKJV

15. https://www.biblegateway.com/passage/?search=1+Corinthians+2%3A11+&version=NKJV

16. https://www.biblegateway.com/passage/?search=John+16%3A13+&version=NKJV

what to say, how to say it, and when to say it, "But the Helper, the Holy Spirit, whom the Father will send in my name, he will teach you all things and bring to your remembrance all that I have said to you" (John 14:26 NKJV[17]).

At the end of the book of Matthew, the disciples were given special instructions by Jesus, ones that would change the world forever as they knew it. Jesus said, "Go ye therefore, and make disciples of all the nations, baptizing them into the name of the Father, and of the Son and the Holy Spirit" (Matthew 28:19[18] NKJV). This commission was not only for the disciples of that day but for all those who follow Christ today. Are you filled with the spirit of God? Are you making disciples of others?

Names and Titles of the Holy Spirit:

Below are a few of the many names for which the Holy Spirit is known. They denote many of the functions and aspects of His ministry:

a. Comforter / Counselor / Helper / Advocate: (Isaiah 11:2[19] NKJV; John 14:16; 15:26; 16:7[20])
b. Intercessor: (Romans 8:26[21] NKJV)
c. Author: (2 Peter 1:21[22] NKJV; 2 Timothy 3:16[23])
d. The Lord / Spirit of God / Christ: (Matthew 3:16[24] NKJV; 2 Corinthians 3:17[25]; 1 Peter 1:11[26])

---

17. https://www.biblegateway.com/passage/?search=John+14%3A26+&version=NKJV

18. https://www.biblegateway.com/passage/?search=Matthew+28%3A19&version=NKJV

19. https://www.biblegateway.com/passage/?search=Isaiah+11%3A2&version=NKJV

20. https://www.biblegateway.com/

    passage/?search=John+14%3A16%3B+15%3A26%3B+16%3A7&version=NKJV

21. https://www.biblegateway.com/passage/?search=Romans+8%3A26&version=NKJV

22. https://www.biblegateway.com/passage/?search=2+Peter+1%3A21&version=NKJV

23. https://www.biblegateway.com/passage/?search=2+Timothy+3%3A16&version=NKJV

24. https://www.biblegateway.com/passage/?search=Matthew+3%3A16&version=NKJV

25. https://www.biblegateway.com/passage/?search=2+Corinthians+3%3A17&version=NKJV

26. https://www.biblegateway.com/passage/?search=1+Peter+1%3A11&version=NKJV

    e. Spirit of Truth: (John 14:17; 16:13[27]; 1 Corinthians 2:12-16[28] <u>NKJV</u>)

    f. Witness: (Romans 8:16[29] <u>NKJV</u>; Hebrews 2:4; 10:15[30])

    g. Spirit of Life: (Romans 8:2[31] <u>NKJV</u>)

    h. Teacher: (John 14:26[32] <u>NKJV</u>; 1 Corinthians 2:13[33])

27. https://www.biblegateway.com/passage/?search=John+14%3A17%3B+16%3A13&version=NKJV

28. https://www.biblegateway.com/passage/?search=1+Corinthians+2%3A12-16&version=NKJV

29. https://www.biblegateway.com/passage/?search=Romans+8%3A16&version=NKJV

30. https://www.biblegateway.com/passage/?search=Hebrews+2%3A4%3B+10%3A15&version=NKJV

31. https://www.biblegateway.com/passage/?search=Romans+8%3A2&version=NKJV

32. https://www.biblegateway.com/passage/?search=John+14%3A26&version=NKJV

33. https://www.biblegateway.com/passage/?search=1+Corinthians+2%3A13&version=NKJV

The Holy Spirit: Quiz

1. The term Ghost is changed to what term today?

2. Name the Godhead Trinity.

3 What are some of the names/titles of the Holy Spirit?

4. The Book of Acts is also known as the Book of the ______________,

5. How are heavenly things revealed to man?

6. Regarding speaking up at the right time, who gives the power to speak the right things at the right time?

7. How was John the Baptist related to Jesus?

8. Who was John the Baptist's mother?

9. What was Jesus' commission to the disciples before He left earth?

10. Are you filled with the spirit of God?

Notes to Self:

48

Tongues

Speaking in tongues is the ability (gift) to speak in a language (an unknown language or heavenly language) other than your own at a time when God's spirit moves upon you.

The introduction of tongues is first seen in the Book of Acts, or the Book of the Holy Spirit, on the Day of Pentecost (Acts 2:1-4[1] NKJV). This was the very first occurrence of any such event. After the 120, including the disciples of Jesus, all were assembled and praying in the upper room, an area used for banquets and weddings, of a house borrowed by the disciples. The Bible says, "And suddenly there came a sound from heaven as of a rushing mighty wind, and it filled all the house where they were sitting. 3 And there appeared unto them cloven tongues like as of fire, and it sat upon each of them. 4 And they were all filled with the Holy Ghost and began to speak with other tongues, as the Spirit gave them utterance" (Acts 2:2-4 NKJV[2]).

In Greek, tongues are translated as *languages*, which should bring a better understanding of why they are called tongues. Speaking in tongues was considered a miracle since the people filled with the gift were Hebrew and had no formal training in other languages, "And they were all amazed and marveled, saying one to another, 'Behold, are not all these which speak Galileans? And how hear we every man in our tongue, wherein we were born. The wonderful works of God?'" (Acts 2:7-11[3]).

Growing up in church, I learned that to be filled with the Holy Spirit, one must speak in tongues. This type of teaching came with the following question, "was one not filled with the Holy Spirit if they did not speak in tongues after

---

1. https://www.biblegateway.com/passage/?search=Acts+2%3A1-4&version=NKJV

2. https://www.biblegateway.com/passage/?search=Acts+2%3A2-4&version=NKJV

3. https://www.biblegateway.com/passage/?search=Acts+2%3A7-11+&version=NKJV

they were saved?" The speaking in tongues during the time of the Apostles was for the benefit of those who did not know of Christ and what He did while he was on earth. The ability to speak another language to a person in their native language was a gift from God to declare His mighty works. It was for the benefit of the one hearing the message of God in their native tongue with no interpreter needed. It was required to edify the church. Paul said, "Now, brothers, if I come to you speaking in tongues, how will I benefit you unless I bring you some revelation or knowledge or prophecy or teaching?" (1 Corinthians 14:6 English Standard V[4]ersion). In other words, what benefit is it to those who do not know what is being said unless it's in their language? Therefore, it is called a gift of interpreting tongues. The person speaking the message of God can then be understood by someone who has been given the gift to interpret to those listening, "Do all possess gifts of healing? So, all speak with tongues? Do all interpret?" (1 Cor. 12:30 ESV[5]). There is no confusion about this: if God is going to use someone to speak for Him, then He will give the gift to someone to interpret His message, "For this reason, anyone who speaks in a tongue should pray that he may interpret what he says" (1 Cor. 14:13 ESV[6]).

Some religions may think that the gift of tongues has ceased, and tongues do not seem to occur today in the same manner as they did in the New Testament (1 Cor. 13:8-12[7]); God is still performing these miracles today (1 Cor. 1:7[8]). True, it may not be as prevalent as when the Holy Spirit fell on the Day of Pentecost; however, God is still God and His Spirit still move in a significant way—man changes, not God. Do not believe the hype that speaking tongues is no longer needed in the church, "For God is not a God of confusion but of peace. As in all the churches of the saints" (1 Cor. 12:11 ESV[9]).

---

4. https://www.biblegateway.com/passage/?search=1+Corinthians+14%3A6+&version=ESV

5. https://www.biblegateway.com/passage/?search=1+Corinthians+12%3A30+&version=ESV

6. https://www.biblegateway.com/passage/?search=1+Corinthians+14%3A13+&version=ESV

7. https://www.biblegateway.com/passage/?search=1+Corinthians+13%3A8-12&version=ESV

8. https://www.biblegateway.com/passage/?search=1+Corinthians+1%3A7&version=ESV

9. https://www.biblegateway.com/passage/?search=1+Cor.+12%3A11+&version=ESV

The Jehovah's Witness teachings claim tongues have ceased because "tongues were passed on to other Christians in the presence of the apostles, usually by the apostles by placing their hands on them" (Acts 8: 18; 10:44-46[10] _ESV_). "It appears that those who received the gifts of the spirit from the apostles did not transfer them to others" (Acts 8: 5-7, 14-17[11]). Their illustration is: "A government official may issue a driver's license to someone, but that person is not given the legal authority to issue a license to anyone else. Speaking in tongues ended with the death of the apostles and those who had personally received the gift from them." (JW.ORG[12]). These claims are false. For one, speaking in tongues did not die with the apostles, and two, the apostles did not give their followers the gift of speaking in tongues. The Bible is apparent in how this gift was given, "And these signs will accompany (follow) those who believe... they will speak in new tongues" (Mark 16:17 NIV[13]). If the tongues died when the apostles died, how are many today being given this spiritual gift? If you believe, you too can be gifted with speaking in tongues. This is one way that God audibly speaks to the church today. The Jehovah's Witness teachings also claim, "The miraculous gift of speaking in tongues evidently ended about the end of the first century C.E. _No one today_ [emphasis added] can rightly claim to speak in tongues by God's power." (JW.ORG[14]) This statement is unfounded and false.

Therefore, studying the word of God is imperative and is being led by His spirit into all truth. It is very easy to be misled if you are not in His word and praying for the Holy Spirit to reveal to you what is right and true. "Study to shew thyself approved unto God, a workman that needeth not to be ashamed, rightly dividing the word of truth" (2 Timothy 2:15 KJV[15]). Many believe speaking in tongues has ceased, "Love never fails. But where there are prophecies, they will cease; where there are tongues, they will be still; whether there be knowledge, it will pass away" (1 Cor. 13:8 NIV[16]). Even some Christian leaders today

---

10. https://www.biblegateway.com/passage/?search=Acts+8%3A+18%3B+10%3A44-46&version=ESV

11. https://www.biblegateway.com/passage/?search=Acts+8%3A+5-7%2C+14-17&version=ESV

12. https://www.jw.org/en/bible-teachings/questions/speaking-in-tongues/

13. https://www.biblegateway.com/passage/?search=Mark+16%3A17+&version=NLV

14. https://www.jw.org/en/bible-teachings/questions/speaking-in-tongues/

15. https://www.biblegateway.com/passage/?search=2+Timothy+2%3A15+&version=KJV

are teaching that speaking in tongues has ceased. Where in the word of God does it prove, without a shadow of a doubt, that the Gift that God gives and keeps on giving has ceased? Yes, there will be a time when all of what was written regarding this scripture will cease, but that time has not come yet because Christ has not returned. If there will be sinners, the gift of speaking will continue. For this reason, the gift of tongues was given, "In the Law, it is written: 'With other tongues and through the lips of foreigners I will speak to this people, but even then they will not listen to me, says the Lord.' 22 Tongues, then, are a sign, not for believers but for unbelievers; prophecy, however, is not for unbelievers but believers" (1 Cor. 14:21-22 NIV[17]).

Our society has become increasingly wicked, thus causing God to move less and less amongst His people. In the Bible, sin was the cause of God's silence. And if our world does not heed those same warnings, we, too, will lose the voice of God. Sometimes, even David felt that God was distant: "Why, Lord, do you stand far off? Why do you hide yourself in times of trouble?" (Psalm 10:1 NIV[18]). However, David realized that God was still with him, "You, Lord, hear the desire of the afflicted; you encourage them, and you listen to their cry" (v.17[19]).

There is so much to be said regarding the use of tongues and how the idea of tongues is being misused today simply because of constant erring in certain Christian circles. The Holy Spirit came for two reasons: to edify the Body of Christ and glorify God. As mentioned in the Bible, speaking in tongues is not a necessary sign of salvation. Instead, salvation is achieved by grace through faith, "For by grace are ye saved through faith; and that not of yourselves: *it is* the gift of God" (Ephesians 2:8 KJV[20]). Yes, some in the early church spoke in tongues the moment they became Christians, but not all spoke because God does not give the gift of tongues to everyone (Acts 2:4; 10:46; 19:6[21] KJV). Remember what Paul wrote to the Corinthian church in 1 Cor. 12:4-11, 28-31 NIV[22].

---

16. https://www.biblegateway.com/passage/?search=1+Corinthians+13%3A8&version=NIV

17. https://www.biblegateway.com/passage/?search=1+Corinthians+14%3A21-22&version=NIV

18. https://www.biblegateway.com/passage/?search=Psalm+10%3A1+&version=NIV

19. https://www.biblegateway.com/passage/?search=Psalm+10%3A17&version=NIV

20. https://www.biblegateway.com/passage/?search=Ephesians+2%3A8&version=KJV

Many early Christians had received the gift of tongues and did not understand how it was appropriately used when gathered together. The tongues were a gift from God to those who believed and to aid in the building and edifying of the Body of Christ, which is the Church.

So, even though a sign for salvation is not speaking in tongues, speaking in tongues is indeed a sign, as in the fruit of the Spirit (Galatians 5:22-23[23] NKJV). There are three types of divisions in the use of speaking in tongues: First, there is the private prayer language you use to pray while laying before God in your private prayer time (in your prayer closet). This type of prayer language is not interpreted. The prayer closet lets you open up to God and cry out privately. It's where you can talk and spiritually strategize against the enemy. In the natural, wars are fought and won on the battlefield; in the spiritual, wars are fought and won in prayer, inside your *war room*. (as an aside, the movie War Room is highly recommended). Second, the tongue that is interpreted is defined as proper usage within the church. For example, when the spirit of God falls upon a person in a church setting, and they begin to speak in God's heavenly language, God then provides another to interpret what He has spoken. But there are times when there may be no one present to interpret, and the person speaking in tongues interprets God's message. That's the gift of interpretation in effect. And third, there is the tongue of missionary context. This appears in the word during evangelism, just as in the New Testament, where people present the gospel to those who speak another language and hear God's message in their native tongue. It was appropriate during the time of the apostles because as they ministered to outer regions, they had to be able to share the gospel in other languages. Thus, the gift of speaking in tongues was very prominent in the New Testament and is still very well-known today.

Every true believer of Christ should want and desire to be filled in such a way that they are overcome with the spirit of God and able to speak in tongues. It's a language that you can practice in your prayer closet. The more you speak in

---

21. https://www.biblegateway.com/
    passage/?search=Acts+2%3A4%3B+10%3A46%3B+19%3A6&version=KJV

22. https://www.biblegateway.com/passage/?search=1+Corinthians+12%3A4-11%2C+28-31&version=NIV

23. https://www.biblegateway.com/passage/?search=Galatians+5%3A22-23&version=NKJV

your heavenly language, the more you will be used to doing so. It's a language the devil cannot understand and will be unable to eavesdrop on your petitioning to God. The gift of speaking in tongues is yours for the asking; ask and speak with the tongues of heaven.

Tongues: Quiz

1. When did "tongues" first appear to man?

2. In the Greek, tongues are translated as ______________________.

3. To be filled with the Holy Spirit, one must speak in tongues. (True or False).

4. The gift of tongues has ceased today? (True or False).

5. What are two reasons mentioned that the Holy Spirit was given?

a.

b.

6. How are you saved, according to the Bible? (Eph. 2:8)

7 What are the three different types of tongues used?

a.

b.

c.

8. What is the importance of speaking in tongues?

9. What are the Jehovah's Witnesses' beliefs about the Gift of Tongues?

10. Have you spoken in tongues? Do you believe it is essential to do?

Notes to Self:

Heaven

In the beginning, God created the heavens and the earth

(Genesis 1:1 ESV).

In my Father's house are many rooms. If it were not so, would I have told you that I go to prepare a place for you? (John 14:2 ESV).

Heaven! According to the American Heritage Dictionary (2011). Heaven is defined as "the abode of God, the angels, and the spirits of the righteous after death; the place of state of existence of the blessed after the mortal life."

Q: What is heaven?

A: It is the dwelling place of God

The word heaven is said to be found in the New Testament 276 times. Now, that would be an excellent homework assignment for you to see, in the scriptures, the word *heaven*. Did you know that there is, in fact, more than one heaven? If you are a new Christian, this may be news to you, but if you have read and studied any of the apostle Paul's writing, you would remember him saying that he was "caught up to the third heaven" (2 Corinthians 12:2a[1] ESV). Paul said he was caught up in the third heaven, which means there are a couple more existing heavens. The third heaven, where God abodes, is referred to as the "heaven of heavens" in Nehemiah 9:6[2]. In reading the first book of the Bible (Genesis), the first heaven may be referred to as the "sky" or translated as the "firmament" containing the clouds. Birds, "let the...fowl that may fly above the earth in the open firmament of heaven (Genesis 1:20[3] NKJV)". The interstellar (outer space), where the planets, stars, and many other celestial objects exist, is considered the second heaven (Genesis 1:14-20[4]).

---

1. https://www.biblegateway.com/passage/?search=2+Corinthians+12%3A2&version=ESV

2. https://www.biblegateway.com/passage/?search=Nehemiah+9%3A6&version=ESV

3. https://www.biblegateway.com/passage/?search=Genesis+1%3A20&version=NKJV

4. https://www.biblegateway.com/passage/?search=Genesis+1%3A14-20&version=NKJV

Have you ever wondered if heaven was indeed a real place? There are many movies and books written by those who claim they have died and gone to heaven, but not only that, they have come back! My question (as well as many others) is, "why would you come back?". Books like Heaven is for Real by Todd Burpo; In Light of Eternity by Randy Alcorn; Heaven by Randy Alcorn; The Slumber of Christianity by Ted Dekker; Haven: My Father's House by Anne Graham Lotz; The Five People You Meet in Heaven by Mitch Albom; 90 Minutes in Heaven by Don Piper; and I'll Hold You in Heaven by Jack Hayford, these are rated as the top books about heaven (Fairchild, Mary 2018).

Let me ask you this: if you died and went to heaven, would you want to return to this place? I think not. If (I do not doubt) heaven is as beautiful as claimed (which I do not doubt) by those who say they have been there, then why would they come back? Or, maybe it's for us to learn from the personal experience of those who have died, gone to heaven, and have returned that there is a heaven? You would think that just trusting in what the Bible says about heaven is enough to believe there is a place called heaven. In the article *What is Heaven Live?* Rev. Charles Ball said, "Heaven is just as much a place as New York or Chicago." (1998).

Q: What is Heaven?

A: Heaven is a place of fellowship and eternal joy.

In the Bible, we read that the throne of God is, in fact, heaven, Isaiah 66:1 ESV[5]: "Thus says the Lord: 'Heaven is my throne, and the earth is my footstool; what is the house that you would build for me, and what is the place of my rest?'"; Acts 7:48-49[6] NKJV "Yet the Most High does not dwell in houses made by hands, as the prophet says, 49 'Heaven is my throne, and the earth is my footstool. What kind of house will you build for me, says the Lord, or what is the place of my rest?'"; Matthew 5:34-35 NKJV "But I say to you, Do not take an oath at all, either by heaven, for it is the throne of God, 35 or by the earth, for it is his footstool, or by Jerusalem, for it is the city of the great King".

---

5. https://www.biblegateway.com/passage/?search=Isaiah+66%3A1&version=ESV

6. https://www.biblegateway.com/passage/?search=Acts+7%3A48-49+&version=NKJV

When Jesus ascended back to heaven (Acts 1:9-12[7] ESV), He entered into heaven itself, not one made by hands or an artificial copy of a sanctuary to look like heaven (Hebrews 9:24[8] ESV). Jesus' heavenly ministry is serving on our behalf as our high priest. God Himself made in the only true tabernacle (Hebrews 6:19-20; 8:1-2[9] ESV). One of the most quoted verses, especially during funerals, is John 14:1-4[10] ESV, "Let not your hearts be troubled. Believe in God; believe in me. 2 In my Father's house are many rooms. If it were not so, would I have told you that I go to prepare a place for you? 3 And if I go and prepare a place for you, I will come again and take you to myself, that where I am, you may be also. 4 And you know the way to where I am going". Jesus was preparing His disciples for His departure; they were heart and spirit sad. He encouraged them not to be unhappy because He would no longer be with them. But He was going away to prepare a glorious place for them to be with Him when He returned (John 14:3[11] ESV). Excellent how these verses are favorite readings for funerals today, for Christians and non-Christians alike.

In all the events leading up to this point in John 14[12] ESV, Jesus has been teaching, instructing, healing the sick, raising the dead, and preparing them for His upcoming death. The disciples were confused about why He had to go and leave them behind and why they could not follow Him. In consoling them, Jesus revealed a greater understanding of Himself. Can you imagine hanging out with a friend, being mentored for three and a half years, learning how to be successful in all areas of life only to have them up and tell you that they are leaving, by way of death, but not to be troubled because he would come back? Your thoughts would be confused and complexed as well. Jesus told His disciples, "Let not let your heart be troubled" (John 14:1 NJKV[13]); this is the love of a Good Shepherd. He is comforting His sheep who are troubled in their hearts. What better way to say *you can trust me?* When He said, "You believe in

---

7. https://www.biblegateway.com/passage/?search=Acts+1%3A9-12&version=ESV

8. https://www.biblegateway.com/passage/?search=Hebrews+9%3A24&version=ESV

9. https://www.biblegateway.com/passage/?search=Hebrews+6%3A19-20%3B+8%3A1-2&version=ESV

10. https://www.biblegateway.com/passage/?search=John+14%3A1-4&version=ESV

11. https://www.biblegateway.com/passage/?search=John+14%3A3&version=ESV

12. https://www.biblegateway.com/passage/?search=John+14&version=ESV

13. https://www.biblegateway.com/passage/?search=John+14%3A1&version=NKJV

God, also believe in Me,". This was the solution to their troubled hearts of Him leaving them behind. What better way to say, "you can trust me?". Though Jesus would not be with them, He assured them that whatever He told them in the past three and a half years together, He would accomplish it.

How in the world could the disciples continue the work without Jesus with them? They were fearful and perplexed in their hearts; their Lord and Savior were soon to leave them. Here are parts of the conversations and questions they had with Jesus (John 14 NJKV[14]):

Thomas: "We do not know why you are going; how can we know the way?" (v.5[15]).

Jesus: "I am the way, the truth, and the life. No one comes to the Father except through Me" (v.6[16]).

Philip: "Show us the Father, that is sufficient" (v.8[17]).

Jesus: "Have I been with you so long, and yet you have not known Me, Phillip? He who has seen Me has seen the Father" (v.9[18]).

Q: Where is heaven?

A: Heaven is wherever God is.

The disciples wanted to know what was going on and why. Thomas was upset about what was happening and not knowing the way. "How can we know the way if we don't know where you are going?" That night, they did not understand how they would do anything without Jesus being present. His work on earth was done, He was finished, and it was time for Him to leave and go back to the place from which He came heaven. God's word still comforts our hearts today, reminding us not to be troubled by all that is going on in this world because someday, the return of Christ will be worth it. Since the

---

14. https://www.biblegateway.com/passage/?search=John+14&version=NKJV

15. https://www.biblegateway.com/passage/?search=John+14%3A5&version=NKJV

16. https://www.biblegateway.com/passage/?search=John+14%3A6&version=NKJV

17. https://www.biblegateway.com/passage/?search=John+14%3A8&version=NKJV

18. https://www.biblegateway.com/passage/?search=John+14%3A9&version=NKJV

beginning of time and the fall of man, we have yearned and longed to return home to our Creator. Like Jesus, this is not our home; the inner man desires to be with God. The fantastic thing about all of this is that most Americans (at least 82%) who believe there is a heaven indeed expect to go there when they die, according to Pew Research Center's 2014 Religious Landscape Study[19]. Yet, many of them don't want to die right now to get there. People want to go to heaven but do not want to live a life guaranteeing their safe passage there. The Bible clearly instructs us how to and by whom we must go through to get to heaven.

Here's some help, just in case you need it. Jesus said He was the only authentic way to the Father, "No one comes to the Father, except through Me" (John 14:6 NIV[20]). That pretty much settles any other claims that may say otherwise. Our citizenship is, in fact, in heaven. Paul affirms this in his letter to the Philippian church, "But our citizenship is in heaven. And we eagerly await a Savior from there, the Lord Jesus Christ" (Philippians 3:20 NIV[21]). It is our hope, as believers, to make heaven our new home; Paul wrote, "the faith and love that spring from the hope stored up for you in heaven and about which you have already heard in the true message of the gospel" (Colossians 1:5[22]).

We have all heard *that to be absent from the body means to be present with the Lord*. It is paraphrased from, "Therefore we are always confident, knowing that, while we are at home in the body, we are absent from the Lord: 7 (For we walk by faith, not by sight:) 8 Yes, we are of good courage, and we would rather be away from the body and at home with the Lord. 9 So whether we are at home or away, we make it our aim to please him" (2 Corinthians 5:6-9 ESV[23]). Our only focus and goal should be to see God face-to-face in our new home, heaven.

---

19. https://www.pewforum.org/2015/11/03/u-s-public-becoming-less-religious/

20. https://www.biblegateway.com/passage/?search=John+14%3A6+&version=NIV

21. https://www.biblegateway.com/passage/?search=Philippians+3%3A20+&version=NIV

22. https://www.biblegateway.com/passage/?search=Colossians+1%3A5&version=NIV

23. https://www.biblegateway.com/passage/?search=2+Corinthians+5%3A6-9+&version=ESV

Heaven: Quiz

1. Do you believe that there is a place called heaven?

2. Who made heaven?

3. Where is it found in the Bible?

4. Where is it found in the Bible that there are many mansions in heaven?

5. What is the only way we can get to the Father in heaven?

6. Where is our true "citizenship" located?

7. What is heaven?

8. Where is heaven?

9. How many times is heaven found in the New Testament?

10. What is, and should be, our focus and goal in life as Christians?

Notes to Self:

63

Hell

And fear not them which kill the body but are not able to kill the soul:

But rather fear him which is able to destroy both soul and body in hell.

(Matthew 10:28 New King James Version)

"Go to hell!" Have you ever heard that being spewed out of the mouth of an angry individual? Or maybe that irate person was you. Have you ever told someone to go to hell? Let's be very clear: as real as heaven is, make no mistake, hell is just as absolute! Hell is real, so it's exceptionally bad when you get mad and tell people to go to hell. Never once have I heard anyone tell someone to go to heaven. Why not? Because all we hear about heaven is how lovely, peaceful, and beautiful a place it is. Hell, on the other hand, is depicted by sheer anguish and pain, sorrow and grief. Being told to go to hell means that they want you to suffer in a place of conscious and continuous torment.

Amazingly enough, despite the clear teachings of heaven and hell, some people believe in heaven's reality while rejecting the existence of hell. Wishful thinking! The Bible declares the reality of hell, "And death and hell were cast into the lake of fire. This is the second death. 15 And whosoever was not found written in the book of life was cast into the lake of fire" Revelation 20:14-15 NKJV[1]. And John writes, "And I saw a new heaven and a new earth: for the first heaven and the first earth were passed away, and there was no more sea. 2 And I John saw the holy city, new Jerusalem, coming down from God out of heaven, prepared as a bride adorned for her husband" Revelation 21:1-2[2] NKJV. Did you not know that Jesus spent more of His time warning the people of the perils of hell than He did in encouraging people with the hope of heaven? Amazing. It was imperative in His earthly ministry. He did not want to lose not one soul, hence His coming to die on the cross.

Hades is Greek for the Hebrew word *sheol* (place of the dead). Hell is translated ten times in the Bible, and the grave is translated only once, "O death, where is your sting? O grave, where is your victory?" (1 Corinthians 15:55 KJV[3]).

---

1. https://www.biblegateway.com/passage/?search=Revelation+20%3A14-15&version=NKJV

2. https://www.biblegateway.com/passage/?search=Revelation+21%3A1-2+&version=NKJV

Hell is translated from the Greek word Gehenna (Hebrew Valley of Hinnom). Hell means a place of everlasting torment (Matthew 10:28[4]) for the loss of unsaved souls. Hell was never intended for humans. It was created for Satan and his fallen angels (spiritual demonic beings) for rebelling against God and, so, were cast out of heaven. "How you are fallen from heaven, O Day Star, son of Dawn! How you are cut down to the ground, you who laid the nations low!" (Isaiah 14:12 ESV[5]). It must have been swift when Satan and those whom he deceived were kicked out of heaven because even Jesus said, "I saw Satan fall like lightning from heaven" (Luke 10:18 ESV[6]). And in Revelation 9:1[7] KJV, Satan is seen as "a star that had fallen from the sky to earth." Imagine a star shooting across the sky; now, picture it as Satan falling from grace to the earth. But here is a theological mind-binding fact, "And death and hell were cast into the lake of fire. This is the second death. 15 And whosoever was not found written in the book of life was cast into the lake of fire" (Revelation 20:14-15 KJV[8]). This takes the subject of hell to a whole other level.

The Five "I Wills" of Satan and his Fall from Grace: Isaiah 14:13-14[9] KJV

1. I WILL ASCEND INTO HEAVEN
2. I WILL EXALT MY THRONE ABOVE THE STARS OF GOD.
3. I WILL ALSO SIT UPON THE MOUNT OF THE CONGREGATION.
4. I WILL ASCEND ABOVE THE HEIGHTS OF THE CLOUDS.
5. I WILL BE LIKE THE MOST HIGH

Pride = Fall

1. P - Position

---

3. https://www.biblegateway.com/passage/?search=1+Corinthians+15%3A55+&version=KJV

4. https://www.biblegateway.com/passage/?search=Matthew+10%3A28&version=KJV

5. https://www.biblegateway.com/passage/?search=Isaiah+14%3A12+&version=ESV

6. https://www.biblegateway.com/passage/?search=Luke+10%3A18&version=ESV

7. https://www.biblegateway.com/passage/?search=Revelation+9%3A1+&version=KJV

8. https://www.biblegateway.com/passage/?search=Revelation+20%3A14-15+&version=KJV

9. https://www.biblegateway.com/passage/?search=Isaiah+14%3A13-14&version=KJV

2. R - Rule
3. I - Idolized
4. D - Dominion
5. E - Equality

The fall was all based on this one word, "PRIDE." It's the fall of every person driven by power and a will to take over. The Bible says, "Pride goes before destruction, a haughty spirit before a fall" (Proverbs 16:18 NIV[10]). Look at every prideful person in power, and you will find their results were not too good. In every single case, they fell, and great was that fall. Pride is cancerous and has, for centuries, destroyed kingdoms and empires. Pride has caused men to divorce their spouses and walk away from their families. It has ruined friendships, caused more conflicts with nations, causing more wars. Even though pride can have a negative outcome if not controlled, it can also have a positive outcome if appropriately used. For instance, if God has blessed you through your faithfulness with a brand-new house, there is nothing wrong with being proud of that house and taking good care of it because you realize it was a gift and blessing from God.

If you are a new Christian, be proud you were one of the ones God chose. Your one desire should be to one day reign with Christ in heaven. Your one goal in life is living to please your heavenly Father. What does that look like? How can you live a life that is pleasing to God? Well, to start with, find yourself in His word daily. If you don't read the instruction manual, you will never know what is expected of you. Reading the word of God is our way of hearing God speak to us personally. The Bible is filled with love letters written to His children. There are letters of discipline and instructions on how to live a pleasing life here on earth. A wonderfully written book by the apostle Paul addresses living a life pleasing to God, "Finally, then, brethren, we urge and exhort in the Lord Jesus that you should abound more and more, just as you received from us how you ought to walk and to please God" (1 Thessalonians 4:1 NKJV[11]).

---

10. https://www.biblegateway.com/passage/?search=Proverbs+16%3A18&version=NIV

11. https://www.biblegateway.com/passage/?search=1+Thessalonians+4%3A1+&version=KJV

Does God send people to hell? This is a question that many have asked for thousands of years. "If God is so loving, why would God send people to hell?" God does not send anyone to hell! That needs to be repeated: *God does not send anyone to hell!* This is the choice of every created being on earth. And it is a free choice. You do not have to go to hell. But you may ask, "How does one choose to go to hell?" The simplest way to answer this question is *by not choosing to follow the pathway of Christ.* People go to hell because of their sins; this is the free choice (free will) God has given us. He allows us to choose whatever path we want. Choose wisely, my child.

Hell was not created for us (humankind); it was made for Satan and those angels who rebelled against God. "Then he will say to those on his left, 'Depart from me, you cursed, into the eternal fire prepared for the devil and his angels'" (Matthew 25:41 ESV[12]). Humankind goes to hell for the same reason the fallen angels went to hell: for sin, "for all have sinned and fall short of the glory of God" (Romans 3:23 ESV[13]). All because of the sin of Adam, humankind has a sinful nature, "Therefore, just as sin came into the world through one man, and death through sin, and so death spread to all men because all sinned..." (Romans 5:12 ESV[14]). Hell is also referred to as "darkness," and to be honest, any place where God isn't is undoubtedly dark, "Then said the king to the servants, bind him hand and foot, and take him away, and cast him into outer darkness, there shall be weeping and gnashing of teeth" (Matthew 22:13 KJV[15]).

There is good news. Because God is so loving and forgiving, He has made a way for humankind to avoid hell: accepting and trusting in the atonement of His Son, Christ Jesus. By Jesus coming to earth to atone for the sins of man, the punishment of hell has been removed, "Whoever believes and is baptized will be saved, but whoever does not believe will be condemned" (Mark 16:16 ESV[16]). Jesus bore the weight of the whole world's sin upon Himself, "He himself bore our sins in his body on the tree, that we might die to sin and live

---

12. https://www.biblegateway.com/passage/?search=Matthew+25%3A41&version=ESV

13. https://www.biblegateway.com/passage/?search=Romans+3%3A23+&version=ESV

14. https://www.biblegateway.com/passage/?search=Romans+5%3A12+&version=ESV

15. https://www.biblegateway.com/passage/?search=Matthew+22%3A13+&version=KJV

16. https://www.biblegateway.com/passage/?search=Mark+16%3A16+&version=ESV

to righteousness. By his wounds you have been healed" (1 Peter 2:24 ESV[17]). If you have accepted Christ into your heart and you genuinely believe that you have been forgiven from the stain of sin and recused from the punishment that comes from dying with your sins, then going to hell should never enter your mind. And because of this sacrificial and merciful love of Jesus, we have an accessible pathway to Christ, away from hell.

---

17. https://www.biblegateway.com/passage/?search=1+Peter+2%3A24+&version=ESV

Hell: Quiz

1. What is the Greek translation of the Hebrew word sheol?

2. What is the Greek translation word for hell?

3. How was Satan's fall from heaven described?

4. What are the five "I Wills" of Satan, and where are they found?

a.

b.

c.

d.

e.

5. What is the acronym for pride?

a.

b.

c.

d.

e.

6. Why was hell created?

7. Do you believe there is a hell? Yes / No (Explain your answer)

8. How does one go to hell?

9. What/who is our pathway to God?

10. What is the second death? (Rev. 20:14[1])

1. https://www.biblegateway.com/passage/?search=Rev.+20%3A14&version=KJV

Notes to Self:

71

Sin

Whoever commits sin also commits lawlessness, and sin is lawlessness.

(1 John 3:4 NKJV)

Sin is such a small word with a substantial life-altering impact. Sin is the one thing that can separate us from our heavenly Father. It was the one thing that got Adam and Eve banded and kicked out of the garden of Eden, "therefore, the Lord God sent him out from the garden of Eden to work the ground from which he was taken. 24 He drove out the man, and at the east of the garden of Eden, he placed the cherubim and a flaming sword that turned every way to guard the way to the tree of life" (Genesis 3:23-24 ESV[1]). And because of this sin, we all suffer the consequences.

Sin, what is it? Sin is a transgression against the laws of God. It is anything that displeases God—breaking His laws. Disobedience. Rebellion. Throughout the journey of the children of Israel, they rebelled against God, "Remember! Do not forget how you provoked the Lord your God to wrath in the wilderness. From the day that you departed from the land of Egypt unto you came to this place, you have been rebellious against the Lord" (Deuteronomy 9:7 NKJV[2]).

There is a study of sin called the Hamartiology Theology. It is the investigation of the origination of sin and how it affects humankind, the degrees of sin and the many different types of sin, as well as the results of sin. No one knows sin's primary origin or how it manifested everywhere, including heaven. But we do read that as a result of it, Lucifer (now called Satan) was kicked out of heaven for his rebellious pride (Isaiah 14:13-14[3] NKJV). He was on earth before man was created (Luke 1:18[4] NKJV). He had to have seen how God loved His creation; Adam was perfect. That had to have infuriated Satan, and since his fall from grace (heaven), he has been scheming and plotting ways to get back at God and deceive as many people as he can before he is cast into the

---

1. https://www.biblegateway.com/passage/?search=Genesis+3%3A23-24+&version=ESV

2. https://www.biblegateway.com/passage/?search=Deuteronomy+9%3A7+&version=NKJV

3. https://www.biblegateway.com/passage/?search=Isaiah+14%3A13-14&version=NKJV

4. https://www.biblegateway.com/passage/?search=Luke+1%3A18&version=NKJV

lake of fire forever "The devil who had deceived them was cast into the lake of fire and brimstone, where the beast and the false prophet are; and they shall be tormented day and night forever and ever" (Revelation 20:10 NKJV[5]). Isn't it amazing that we all know what the devil's end will be, yet he still works overtime to deceive people?

The Scheme: Temptation, The Fall of Man (Genesis 3[6] <u>NKJV</u>)

In Genesis chapter 3, we are introduced to the serpent, Satan, in fallen form. It is where Satan crafted his plan to deceive man. And it is in the form of what we call temptation. He twisted the truth of God, and even today, that same sin is used to deceive humankind. Satan tricks people into thinking that a lie is true: "Has God indeed said, 'You shall not eat of every tree of the garden'?" (Gen. 3:3[7]b; Gen. 2:16-17[8]). This one question enticed Eve to doubt. Her doubt was then planted into the heart of her husband, Adam, the one God created first, the one that could have stopped it all, and rebuked his wife for bringing this enticing thought of doubt. One can only try to imagine what life would be like if Adam had refused to eat the fruit from the tree of the knowledge of good and evil (Gen. 2:16[9]). And just as God warned them, if they did eat of that tree, they would "surely die" (Gen. 2:17[10]). It wasn't a natural death as one would think, and that's the twisted part of Satan's lie. The fact was that they would not die, but they would be as wise as God, "For God knows that when you eat of it your eyes will be opened, and you will be like God, knowing good and evil" (Gen. 3:5 ESV[11]). It was curiosity that caused Eve to eat the fruit. Curiosity! Is this why secrets can't be kept today? We must know what is forbidden.

Death came, not in the natural sense but in a spiritual sense. That first sin caused man to be separated from God spiritually, and because of man's sin, God placed a curse on all of humankind. He asked Adam, "Why?" he blamed

5. https://www.biblegateway.com/passage/?search=Revelation+20%3A10+&version=NKJV

6. https://www.biblegateway.com/passage/?search=Genesis+3&version=NKJV

7. https://www.biblegateway.com/passage/?search=Genesis+3%3A3&version=NKJV

8. https://www.biblegateway.com/passage/?search=Genesis+2%3A16-17&version=NKJV

9. https://www.biblegateway.com/passage/?search=Genesis+2%3A16&version=NKJV

10. https://www.biblegateway.com/passage/?search=Genesis+2%3A17&version=NKJV

11. https://www.biblegateway.com/passage/?search=Genesis+3%3A5&version=ESV

the woman; he asked the woman, "Why?" and she blamed the serpent (Gen. 3:11-13[12] NKJV). The serpent had no one else to blame, so the Lord God said to the serpent, "Because you have done this, You *are* cursed more than all cattle, And more than every beast of the field; On your belly, you shall go (the birth of the snake), And you shall eat dust All the days of your life" (Gen. 3:14 NKJV[13]). It was promised that the seed of woman, one day, would save humanity from eternal damnation from the consequences of their sin, "And I will put enmity Between you and the woman, And between your seed and her Seed; He shall bruise your head, And you shall bruise His heel" (Gen. 3:14-15 NKJV[14]). But until Jesus was born, earthly consequences of man's sin temporarily remained.

God removed Adam and Eve from the garden, knowing that if He did not, they might eat of the Tree of Life, causing them to live forever, "Then the Lord God said, 'Behold, the man has become like one of Us, to know good and evil. And now, lest he put out his hand and also take of the tree of life, and eat, and live forever— 23, therefore, the Lord God sent him out of the garden of Eden to till the ground from which he was taken. 24 So He drove out the man, and He placed cherubim at the east of the garden of Eden, and a flaming sword which turned every way, to guard the way to the tree of life" (Gen. 3:22-24 NKJV[15]). Not only were Adam and Eve kicked out of the Garden of Eden, they were prevented from ever returning to the perfect place they once knew.

Let's be very clear in our understanding of sin and how all sin has consequences. Even though there may be degrees of sin (and some sins may be more detestable to God), they are all equally the same when it comes to the eternal consequences of sin and are punishable by death. Paul made this point evident when he wrote, "For the wages of sin *is* death, but the gift of God *is* eternal life in Christ Jesus our Lord" (Romans 6:23 NKJV[16]). Sin carries with it condemnation and eternal death in the lake of fire! "For all who do such

---

12. https://www.biblegateway.com/passage/?search=Genesis+3%3A11-13&version=NKJV

13. https://www.biblegateway.com/passage/?search=Genesis+3%3A14+&version=NKJV

14. https://www.biblegateway.com/passage/?search=Genesis+3%3A14-15+&version=NKJV

15. https://www.biblegateway.com/passage/?search=Genesis+3%3A22-24+&version=NKJV

16. https://www.biblegateway.com/passage/?search=Romans+6%3A23+&version=NKJV

things, <u>all who behave unrighteous</u>, *are* an abomination to the Lord your God" (Deuteronomy 25:16 NKJV[17]). You probably didn't know that God hates. Yes, it's true. God hates. There are 117 references in the Bible to the word abomination (references).

Six things the Lord hates:

1. Proud look (Proverbs 16:18[18] <u>NKJV</u>; Daniel 4:37[19]; Jeremiah 50:31[20]; Matthew 23:12[21])
2. Lying tongue (John 8:44[22] <u>NKJV</u>; John 8:32[23])
3. Murder (Exodus 20:13[24] <u>NKJV</u>; 1 John 3:15[25]; Jeremiah 18:18[26])
4. A heart that devises wicked (Matthew 5:28[27] <u>NKJV</u>; Romans 6:23[28])
5. Feet that are swift in running to evil (Psalms 1:1[29] <u>NKJV</u>)
6. One who sows discord among brethren (Ephesians 4:31[30] <u>NKJV</u>; James 1:26[31])

Adam allowed and caused a great curse upon all humanity yet to be born. A true fellowship was broken due to being enticed to disobey God. For centuries, the world has been groaning and crying for natural and spiritual relief, ultimately coming through the redemptive love of Christ's return, "For we

---

17. https://www.biblegateway.com/passage/?search=Deuteronomy+25%3A16+&version=NKJV

18. https://www.biblegateway.com/passage/?search=Proverbs+16%3A18&version=NKJV

19. https://www.biblegateway.com/passage/?search=Daniel+4%3A37&version=NKJV

20. https://www.biblegateway.com/passage/?search=Jeremiah+50%3A31&version=NKJV

21. https://www.biblegateway.com/passage/?search=Matthew+23%3A12&version=NKJV

22. https://www.biblegateway.com/passage/?search=John+8%3A44&version=NKJV

23. https://www.biblegateway.com/passage/?search=John+8%3A32&version=NKJV

24. https://www.biblegateway.com/passage/?search=Exodus+20%3A13&version=NKJV

25. https://www.biblegateway.com/passage/?search=1+John+3%3A15&version=NKJV

26. https://www.biblegateway.com/passage/?search=Jeremiah+18%3A18&version=NKJV

27. https://www.biblegateway.com/passage/?search=Matthew+5%3A28&version=NKJV

28. https://www.biblegateway.com/passage/?search=Romans+6%3A23&version=NKJV

29. https://www.biblegateway.com/passage/?search=Psalms+1%3A1&version=NKJV

30. https://www.biblegateway.com/passage/?search=Ephesians+4%3A31&version=NKJV

31. https://www.biblegateway.com/passage/?search=James+1%3A26&version=NKJV

know that the whole creation has been groaning together in the pains of childbirth until now. 23 And not only the creation, but we, who have the first fruits of the Spirit, groan inwardly as we wait eagerly for adoption as sons, the redemption of our bodies" (Romans 8:22-23 ESV[32]).

As a result of Christ coming to earth, being crucified, dying on the cross, being buried in a grave, only to rise again on the third day, the "fallen" man has redemption of his sin through the shed blood of Jesus Christ. As we know today, all things that are being destroyed by sin will be restored by God upon Christ's return (Acts 3:21[33] NKJV). God said in His word that He would create a new heaven and earth: "For behold, I create new heavens and a new earth, and the former things shall not be remembered or come into mind" (Isaiah 65:17 ESV[34]). Peter wrote, "waiting for and hastening the coming of the day of God, because of which the heavens will be set on fire and dissolved, and the heavenly bodies will melt as they burn! 13 But according to his promise, we are waiting for new heavens and a new earth in which righteousness dwells" (2 Peter 3:12-13 ESV[35]). John witnessed in his vision, "Then I saw a new heaven and a new earth, for the first heaven and the first earth had passed away, and the sea was no more" (Revelation 21:1 ESV[36]).

You, too, can *count yourself dead to sin and alive to God in Christ Jesus if you are born again*, "So you also must consider yourselves dead to sin and alive to God in Christ Jesus" (Revelation 6:11 ESV[37]). You, too, can be free of your sin (Romans 10:9-10[38] ESV).

---

32. https://www.biblegateway.com/passage/?search=Romans+8%3A22-23+&version=NKJV

33. https://www.biblegateway.com/passage/?search=Acts+3%3A21&version=NKJV

34. https://www.biblegateway.com/passage/?search=Isaiah+65%3A17+&version=ESV

35. https://www.biblegateway.com/passage/?search=2+Peter+3%3A12-13+&version=ESV

36. https://www.biblegateway.com/passage/?search=Revelation+21%3A1+&version=ESV

37. https://www.biblegateway.com/passage/?search=Revelation+6%3A11+&version=ESV

38. https://www.biblegateway.com/passage/?search=Romans+10%3A9-10&version=ESV

Sin: Quiz

1. What is sin?

2. What is the study of the origination of sin called?

3. Satan was called_________________, before his fall from heaven.

4. The first sin in the world was due to Satan _________________ Eve.

5. What happened when Adam and Eve ate of the fruit of the knowledge of good and evil?

6. What was man's punishment for eating the fruit? (Genesis 3:23[1]):

7. Satan (the serpent) was turned into what for deceiving man?

8. What are the six things that God hates? (Proverbs 6:16-19[2]):

a.

b.

c.

d.

e.

f.

9. What is an abomination?

10. How can one be made free of sin? (Romans 10:9-10[3]):

---

1. https://www.biblegateway.com/passage/?search=Genesis+3%3A23&version=ESV

2. https://www.biblegateway.com/passage/?search=Proverbs+6%3A16-19&version=ESV

3. https://www.biblegateway.com/passage/?search=Romans+10%3A9-10&version=ESV

Notes to Self:

Salvation

And they said, "Believe in the Lord Jesus, and you will be saved, you and your household.

(Acts 16:31 ESV)

What is salvation? We hear the talk of salvation every single Sunday of the month in church. But what is salvation? How can one obtain salvation? What is the "Plan of salvation" we hear about so often? Well, I am glad you asked because that is what we will discuss in this lesson. I remember my days in Sunday School singing the Salvation song. It went something like this, "Oh, you can't get to heaven without it, S.A.L.V.A.T.I.O.N." It would have to be correctly spelled out. Everyone would stop singing except the person chosen at random (which would be me most of the time) by the Sunday School Superintendent to spell out the word *salvation*. It was rather embarrassing if you didn't know how to spell salvation. So, the song was a great way to learn how to spell salvation. But once we learned how to spell it, we would know what salvation meant.

What is Salvation?

The dictionary defines salvation as "preservation or deliverance from harm, ruin, or loss" (New Dictionary of Cultural Literacy). It's a lifeline, preservation, or conservation. In theology, it's deliverance from sin and its consequences, which Christians believe *to be brought about by faith in Christ*. It's redemption, saving, deliverance, reclamation, help.

The deliverance from suffering and danger, protect and save; that is salvation. It is often used for spiritual deliverance. According to the Bible, there is only one way to be saved or delivered: by Christ Jesus. All of humankind needs salvation. Since the fall of man the Bible declares that no one is righteous and all have sinned, "Surely there is not a righteous man on earth who does good and never sins" (Ecclesiastes 7:20 ESV[1]); "for all have sinned and fall short of the glory of God," (Romans 2:23 ESV[2]); "If we say we have no sin, we deceive ourselves, and the truth is not in us" (1 John 1:8[3] ESV). As we read in the following scriptures,

---

1. https://www.biblegateway.com/passage/?search=Ecclesiastes+7%3A20+&version=ESV

2. https://www.biblegateway.com/passage/?search=Romans+2%3A23++&version=ESV

God alone can remove and deliver us from the penalty of sin, "who has saved us and called *us* with a holy calling, not according to our works, but according to His purpose and grace which was given to us in Christ Jesus before time began" (2 Timothy 1:9[4] ESV); "not by works of righteousness which we have done, but according to His mercy He saved us, through the washing of regeneration and renewing of the Holy Spirit" (Titus 3:5[5]).

How to Obtain Salvation:

How can you be saved and delivered from sin? The Bible says that we are saved by grace through our faith in Christ Jesus, "For by grace you have been saved through faith. And this is not your own doing; it is the gift of God" (Ephesians 2:8 ESV[6]). This is how we obtain salvation, not even by our works. No amount of good deeds will get you into heaven. Isaiah said, "I will expose your righteousness and your works, and they will not benefit you" (Isaiah 57:12[7] ESV). It is only by Jesus and Him alone that salvation is obtained—three things you must do to receive salvation. First, you must hear the good news of Christ Jesus, His crucifixion, His death and burial, and His resurrection, "In him you also, when you heard the word of truth, the gospel of your salvation, and believed in him, were sealed with the promised Holy Spirit" (Ephesians 1:13 ESV[8]). Second, you must believe and fully put your trust in Jesus as your Lord and Savior (Romans 10:10[9]), and not be ashamed of what He did for you by forgiving you from your transgressions, "For I am not ashamed of the gospel, for it is the power of God for salvation to everyone who believes, to the Jew first and also to the Greek" (Romans 1:16 ESV[10]). Lastly, all of this involves you repenting, changing your mind, changing your direction, and going in the direction that God wants you to go: a new pathway to Christ. This pathway

---

3. https://www.biblegateway.com/passage/?search=1+John+1%3A8&version=ESV

4. https://www.biblegateway.com/passage/?search=2+Timothy+1%3A9&version=ESV

5. https://www.biblegateway.com/passage/?search=Titus+3%3A5&version=ESV

6. https://www.biblegateway.com/passage/?search=Ephesians+2%3A8+&version=ESV

7. https://www.biblegateway.com/passage/?search=Isaiah+57%3A12&version=ESV

8. https://www.biblegateway.com/passage/?search=Ephesians+1%3A13+&version=ESV

9. https://www.biblegateway.com/passage/?search=Romans+10%3A10&version=ESV

10. https://www.biblegateway.com/passage/?search=Romans+1%3A16&version=ESV

will deliver you from a pathway of death and destruction. Paul said, "Repent therefore and turn back, that your sins may be blotted out" (Acts 3:19 ESV[11]). Why? Because "For everyone who calls on the name of the Lord will be saved" (Acts 10:13 ESV[12]), that's why.

What is the Plan of Salvation?

We just learned about the three things you must do to obtain salvation. Now, let's talk about the plan of salvation and what that entails. The plan of salvation consists of three basic things: the *why*, the *who,* and the *how*. The most important thing to remember is that this is not humanity's plan, but it is God's plan. The plan of man might consist of observing all types of religious rituals, obeying certain doctrinal beliefs, and achieving some types of spiritual enlightenment, but that's not God's plan of salvation. None of these things can help you receive salvation in God's way.

The Why: (Ecclesiastes 7:20[13] ESV; Romans 3:23[14]; 1 John 1:8[15])

The first thing we need to know and understand about salvation is why we need it. Why do we need to be saved, and what are we saved from? Here's a question I have been asked over the years, and if you are a new believer, you can rest assured that someone you know will ask you this same question, "What did you get saved from?" and this is your perfect opportunity to witness to them how you accepted Christ as your Lord and Savior. He rescued you from the flames of hell to one day live in heaven with Him. This is one great reason why we need to be saved. Sin, as we learned in the section "Sin," is a rebellion against God. Sin is harmful to one's health. It is detrimental to others, can damage relationships, and, most importantly, dishonors God.

The Bible is prominent when it says that God cannot allow sin to go unpunished, being He's a holy and just God. And the punishment for sin is

---

11. https://www.biblegateway.com/passage/?search=Acts+3%3A19+&version=ESV

12. https://www.biblegateway.com/passage/?search=Acts+10%3A13&version=ESV

13. https://www.biblegateway.com/passage/?search=Ecclesiastes+7%3A20&version=ESV

14. https://www.biblegateway.com/passage/?search=Romans+3%3A23&version=ESV

15. https://www.biblegateway.com/passage/?search=1+John+1%3A8&version=ESV

death, "For the wages of sin is death, but the gift of God is eternal life in Christ Jesus our Lord" (Romans 6:23 ESV[16]). And this death and punishment is eternal and a separation from God Himself. The "why" is simple: we need salvation because we are sinners.

> "Then I saw a great white throne and him who was seated on it. From his presence, earth and sky fled away, and no place was found for them. 12 And I saw the dead, great and small, standing before the throne, and books were opened. Then, another book was opened, which is the Book of Life. And the dead were judged by what was written in the books, according to what they had done. 13 And the sea gave up the dead who were in it, Death and Hades gave up the dead who were in them, and they were judged, each one of them, according to what they had done. 14 Then Death and Hades were thrown into the lake of fire. This is the second death, the lake of fire. 15 And if anyone's name was not found written in the book of life, he was thrown into the lake of fire" (Revelation 20:11-15 ESV[17]).

The Who: (Matthew 16:15-16[18]; John 1:1, 14[19])

The "who" referenced here is not the English rock band that started in 1964. Depending on how old you are, you may not have a clue of who it is I am referring to. But the "who" I am talking about is Jesus, the Christ Himself. He is the "who" we will receive the necessary salvation. We cannot save ourselves because of our sins and the consequences that come from them. God became a human being, and (here is the mind-blowing mystery of this) He accomplished this through the Person of His Son Jesus Christ, "In the beginning was the Word, and the Word was with God, and the Word was God..." 14 "And the Word became flesh and dwelt among us, and we have seen his glory, glory as of the only Son from the Father, full of grace and truth" (John 1:1, 14 ESV[20]).

---

16. https://www.biblegateway.com/passage/?search=Romans+6%3A23+&version=ESV

17. https://www.biblegateway.com/passage/?search=Revelation+20%3A11-15+&version=ESV

18. https://www.biblegateway.com/passage/?search=Matthew+16%3A15-16&version=ESV

19. https://www.biblegateway.com/passage/?search=John+1%3A1%2C+14&version=ESV

20. https://www.biblegateway.com/passage/?search=John+1%3A1%2C+14&version=ESV

Jesus was sinless; He lived a very sinless life, offering Himself as a perfect sacrificial lamb on our behalf (2 Corinthians 5:21[21] ESV; Hebrews 4:15[22]; 1 John 3:5[23]; 1 Corinthians 15:3[24]; Colossians 1:22[25]; Hebrews 10:10[26]). Jesus' death, was of infinite and eternal value; why? Because He was God, He died on the cross and paid a debt we could not pay for the sins of the whole world, "He is the propitiation for our sins, and not for ours only but also for the sins of the whole world" (1 John 2:2 ESV[27]). Salvation is available today because of Jesus' resurrection from the dead; it demonstrated that His sacrificial love was indeed enough for salvation.

The How: (Acts 16:31[28] ESV)

When you have heard the good news, and your heart has been convicted, you have an absolute emptiness to be filled. Your heart, mind, and soul want to know, "How do I receive salvation? What must I do to be saved?". This same question was asked of Paul, and his response was, "Believe in the Lord Jesus, and you will be saved, you and your household" (Acts 16:31[29]). This is the most significant "how" in receiving salvation. You must believe in Jesus Christ, Lord and Savior of all, and you will be saved. There is no magic formula, and there are no motivational steps to salvation. Today, people want steps for this, and they want steps for that. There are steps on all types of "how to": how to lose weight, how to be more successful, how to get rich, how to find the right person. All these steps may be fine and dandy in obtaining material goods and motivating people who need mental encouragement. Still, when it comes to salvation, there is only one authentic way (step): through Jesus Christ.

---

21. https://www.biblegateway.com/passage/?search=2+Corinthians+5%3A21&version=ESV

22. https://www.biblegateway.com/passage/?search=Hebrews+4%3A15&version=ESV

23. https://www.biblegateway.com/passage/?search=1+John+3%3A5&version=ESV

24. https://www.biblegateway.com/passage/?search=1+Corinthians+15%3A3&version=ESV

25. https://www.biblegateway.com/passage/?search=Colossians+1%3A22&version=ESV

26. https://www.biblegateway.com/passage/?search=Hebrews+10%3A10&version=ESV

27. https://www.biblegateway.com/passage/?search=1+John+2%3A2+&version=ESV

28. https://www.biblegateway.com/passage/?search=Acts+16%3A31&version=ESV

29. https://www.biblegateway.com/passage/?search=Acts+16%3A31&version=ESV

The mistake many of us make in church leadership is trying to teach a step-by-step process of salvation. The Roman Catholic Church has seven sacraments. Many Christian denominations add public confession, turning from sin, baptism, speaking in tongues, and the list goes on as steps to salvation. In the Islamic faith, there are Five Pillars. Which, if they obey, grant salvation. It is also believed (by some, not all) that if they martyr themselves, 72 virgins[30] are promised to them in paradise. The Bible points out and presents only one step to salvation. What must you do to be saved? Do you know the steps to take? (Acts 16:31[31] ESV; Romans 10:9-10[32]). The Five Pillars of Islam are listed, and what they believe will grant salvation if obeyed.

Five Pillars of Islam:

1. **Shahada:** is the Islamic proclamation that "There is no true God except Allah, and Muhammad is the Messenger of Allah."
2. **Prayer (Salat)**: Confessions of sins. The names of the prayers are Fajr, Dhuhr, Asr, Maghrib, and Isha.
3. **Fasting (Saum)**: For the entire month of Ramadan, there is no drinking, eating, or sexual relations during the daylight hours.
4. **Alms-giving of charity (Zakat)**: To move oneself towards holiness and submission to Allah. It would help if you gave to people experiencing poverty. It is considered a form of worship to God.
5. **Pilgrimage (Hajj)**: Muslims must make the pilgrimage to Mecca in the first half of the last month of the lunar year.

When you truly trust what Jesus has done for us on the cross and in no other works or steps, then that's when righteousness is given to you. Here is the tradeoff: you give your sin to Him, He takes your sin, and He gives you righteousness. Trust in Jesus, believe in Him, obtain salvation, and you will never face the judgment of God, "My sheep hear My voice, and I know them, and they follow Me; 28 and I give eternal life to them, and they will never

---

30. http://www.aviperry.org/political-blogs/where-did-the-notion-of-72-virgins-in-islamic-paradise-come-from

31. https://www.biblegateway.com/passage/?search=Acts+16%3A31&version=ESV

32. https://www.biblegateway.com/passage/?search=Romans+10%3A9-10&version=ESV

perish; and no one will snatch them out of My hand" (John 10:27-28 NIV[33]). Two things distinguish the faith of Christianity from all other religions in the world. One, it's not a religion; it's a relationship with Christ. And two, there are no steps that you must follow to receive salvation. The faith of a Christian recognizes that the steps have already been completed and said; it just calls on the repentant heart, by faith, to receive Him.

---

33. https://www.biblegateway.com/passage/?search=John+10%3A27-28&version=ESV

Salvation: Quiz

1. What is the definition of salvation?

2. Who is the only one who can save and deliver you from sin?

3. What two things must you do to obtain salvation?

a.

b.

4. The plan of salvation consists of three things: what are they?

a.

b.

c.

5. What are the Five Pillars of Islam?

a.

b.

c.

d.

e.

6. Two things that distinguish the Christian faith from other religions are:

a.

b.

7. God requires five steps to be granted salvation (True or False).

8. God must punish the sinner (True or False).

9. Salvation is a gift you must work for (True or False).

10. Salvation is found in only one way, how?

Notes to Self:

88

Baptism

Peter replied, "Repent and be baptized, every one of you, in the name of Jesus Christ for the forgiveness of your sins. And you will receive the gift of the Holy Spirit.

(Acts 2:38 NIV)

To baptize to *immerse* in water, but first and foremost, let's address this one fact right out the gate: baptism is an outward, not an inward, proclamation of the conversion on the inside. We need to understand this because there has been more controversial rhetoric in Acts 2:38[1] regarding whether or not baptism is required for salvation. As we just learned, the one requirement for salvation is Jesus Christ, not baptism. Many teach using this verse, "Then Peter said to them, 'Repent, and let every one of you is baptized in the name of Jesus Christ for the remission of sins, and you shall receive the gift of the Holy Spirit'" that to be saved, one must be baptized. This verse and other verses used to teach salvation do not teach baptismal regeneration (that baptism is necessary for salvation or that baptism saves).

Don't be fooled by this baptismal regeneration doctrine. It is essential to know that with all the doctrines in our society, rarely are they generated from a single verse. To fully understand what God's word means concerning a specific topic, we need to look at and examine all of God's word, not just one verse that fits a present-day movement. There are three exceptional ways to explore the word of God without going too deep into this (because it would have to be examined in a theology course to do this justice).

1. Examine its covenant context.

2. Examine its arrangement, grammar, and structure.

3. Examine its dealings with forgiveness of sins.

God's word commanded all people to repent of their sins. John the Baptist preached this day and night in the back deserts of Judaea (Matthew 3[2] NKJV).

---

1. https://www.biblegateway.com/passage/?search=Acts+2%3A38&version=NKJV

2. https://www.biblegateway.com/passage/?search=Matthew+3&version=NKJV

John preached repentance and baptized as many as would be baptized. He told the people that he baptized them with water unto repentance (Matthew 3:11[3]), but there was one coming that would baptize them with the Holy Ghost and with fire, which came to pass on the day of Pentecost (Acts 2:3[4] NKJV).

Taking the message of John to heart, the people would believe and repent; thus, the new Christian would be baptized. This is the outward identification of becoming a new believer (new convert, new creation) who has already repented. Acts 2:38[5] NKJV does not demonstrate that baptism is essential to receive salvation. It is the one thing we receive to identify ourselves publicly with Christ. It is the inward manifestation of the work that God has completed within us.

Even if you never attend a Bible college (although I hope you would), consider taking a course or two in religious studies (theology). It would be a great experience to learn about all types of religious studies, accounting, and economics. I believe that well-rounded study brings a good balance into your life spiritually and naturally. But even if you take biblical courses, you will never find an entry in the Bible stating that we are justified by grace and baptism. Nowhere will you find that we are saved by faith and baptism. But you will find that the Bible says we are saved by grace through faith, "For it is by grace you have been saved, through faith and this is not from yourselves, it is the gift of God" (Ephesians 2:8 NIV[6]).

As you will learn in your biblical studies, baptism is excluded from the gospel messages. Regarding this topic, Paul said in 1 Corinthians: "I thank God that I did not baptize any of you except Crispus and Gaius, 15 so no one can say that you were baptized in my name. 16 (Yes, I also baptized the household of Stephanas; beyond that, I don't remember if I baptized anyone else.) 17 For Christ did not send me to baptize, but to preach the gospel—not with wisdom and eloquence, lest the cross of Christ be emptied of its power" (1 Corinthians 1:14-17 NIV[7]).

---

3. https://www.biblegateway.com/passage/?search=Matthew+3%3A11&version=NKJV

4. https://www.biblegateway.com/passage/?search=Acts+2%3A3&version=NKJV

5. https://www.biblegateway.com/passage/?search=Acts+2%3A38+&version=NKJV

6. https://www.biblegateway.com/passage/?search=Ephesians+2%3A8+&version=NIV

Paul's message was clear: it was not about baptism. It was about the gospel, the resurrection of Christ. He wrote this in 1 Corinthians 15:1-4[8], "Now, brothers and sisters, I want to remind you of the gospel I preached to you, which you received and on which you have taken your stand. 2 This gospel saves you if you hold firmly to the word I preached to you. Otherwise, you have believed in vain. 3 For what I received I passed on to you as of first importance: that Christ died for our sins according to the Scriptures, that he was buried, that he was raised on the third day according to the Scriptures." As you can see, Paul did not include baptism in the definition of the gospel. Baptism is not what saves us. Baptism is not part of salvation and is not necessary for salvation. Baptism is an act of what someone does who is already saved.

---

7. https://www.biblegateway.com/passage/?search=1+Corinthians+1%3A14-17+&version=NIV

8. https://www.biblegateway.com/passage/?search=1+Corinthians+15%3A1-4&version=NIV

Baptism: Quiz

1. What does baptism mean?

2. Explain what baptism is.

3. How did John baptize?

4. How did Jesus baptize?

5. Does one have to be baptized to receive salvation? ______ Why or why not?

6. This was excluded totally out of the gospel message: ____________________.

7. What was Paul's message about?

8. What was Paul's message not about?

9. Baptism is what someone does who is already saved (True or False).

10. Have you been baptized?

Notes to Self:

Pathway to Christ

Jesus said to him, "I am the way, and the truth, and the life. No one comes to the Father except through me."

(John 14:6 ESV)

Before Christ, what was the pathway to salvation? As confusing as this question may seem to many, I will ask it anyway: have you ever thought about how people were saved in the Old Testament era? Reading the New Testament, we know salvation comes through grace and faith in Christ Jesus. And we also become the children of God (John 1:12[1] ESV; Ephesians 2:8-9[2]).

There are many pathways in life, as you may know. And the path you take in life can either take you to success or failure. How do you determine which pathway you should take? As a child, your parents try to guide or dictate the path you should take. Like most children, you may not listen or choose to take their route, but it's not your desire or dream. And your path should be one thing you choose (as long as it does not harm anyone). If you are pleased and your path brings joy, follow your heart and live your dreams fully. Don't allow anyone to hinder your course to happiness. You have one life. You don't get a do-over. So, choose your pathway wisely.

To live a life on purpose should bring such joy because the rules and regulations of man do not bind you. You are living a life that God has designed and created for you. In the book of Jeremiah, the prophet writes, "'For I know the plans I have for you' declares the Lord, 'plans to prosper you and not to harm you, plans to give you hope and a future'" (Jeremiah 29:11 NKJV[3]). Sometimes, we want to hear that God will prosper and make us rich. We want to hear that He will move us from where we are to where we desire: in a big home, fantastic job, great car, etc. But what about what God meant in his verse? What about the preceding verses that tell a different story? A story that tells us to stay right where we are until those cursing and doing us wrong are blessed, and then we

---

1. https://www.biblegateway.com/passage/?search=John+1%3A12&version=ESV

2. https://www.biblegateway.com/passage/?search=Ephesians+2%3A8-9&version=ESV

3. https://www.biblegateway.com/passage/?search=Jeremiah+29%3A11&version=NKJV

will be blessed? Oh no! That is not in "our plans"; that can't be what God is saying!

That is what happened to the Israelites. Therefore, examining the context of what we read in the word of God is essential. Things become a lot clearer. It is not to say that we will not be blessed, but it is to say that within our blessings, there are some hard lessons to be learned. We just read that there are plans to prosper you, not harm you, and *give you hope and a future.* And there isn't anything wrong with that, per se. We don't want to hear that we must suffer a little to receive that blessing. I know I don't. I believe I have suffered enough in life already, and I am ready for the blessings that God has promised me. Why should I have to suffer anymore? That's not fair. Have you thought this, too? *I'm tired of people holding me back and stealing what rightfully belongs to me.* But the one thing I have learned thus far is that *life is unfair.* That's right. I admit it isn't, and I am shouting it as loudly as possible. *LIFE IS NOT FAIR!* Can I get an Amen? Have I got a witness?!

Here is the other side of that unfairness that I have come to know very well, and it has been somewhat of a mantra of mine down through the years, "No weapon that is formed against me will prosper" (Isaiah 54:17[4] KJV). This verse has comforted me much more than I can share. However, one example I will share happened when I was going through my first divorce; yes, I did say the first divorce (there have been a total of 3; a story for another time and another book). Even though life is not fair and unpleasant sometimes, this verse is my reassurance that it will not always be that way. The verse did not say that I wouldn't have bad days, but it said it would not prosper. It did not say that I would not be disappointed; it said it would not prosper. It did not say that I would not have the money for rent or bills, but it said that it would not prosper. So, what does that tell you? It tells you that problems, hardship, heartaches, and disappointments will happen, but the wonderful part about it is that it will not always last. And there is an end.

So many verses are taken out of context, and it hurts the body of Christ. I am genuinely sorry to have to tell you this, primarily if you use Jeremiah 29:11[5]

---

4. https://www.biblegateway.com/passage/?search=Isaiah+54%3A17&version=NKJV

5. https://www.biblegateway.com/passage/?search=Jeremiah+29%3A11&version=NKJV

for the sole purpose of reaping prosperity. Jeremiah 29:11[6] is not to be used as a security blanket. The context of the verse is this: The Israelites were exiled by Babylon as punishment for their disobedience. The false prophet Hananiah boldly proclaimed the freedom of the Israelites from Babylon in two years. Jeremiah (true prophet of God) confronted Hananiah for lying to the people and falsely proclaiming their early release from bondage. Hananiah lied, and Jeremiah called him out about it. This is the paraphrased version of what Jeremiah said, *"Hananiah. God has a plan for the Israelites, and it is indeed a plan that will give His people hope and a prospering future."* However! Before he shared that promise, Jeremiah gave the Israelites God's directive, "And seek the peace of the city where I have caused you to be carried away captive and pray to the Lord for it; for in its peace you will have peace" (Jeremiah 29:7 NKJV[7]). This was not what the Israelites wanted to hear. They did not want to be told that they had to stay right there and help prosper the nation that had enslaved them. But God did command that. In verse 10, God says, "For thus says the Lord: <u>After seventy years are completed at Babylon</u>, I will visit you and perform My good word toward you and cause you to return to this place." Seriously! After seventy years? They wanted to hear that they were going home. They also wanted to hear that all their suffering had finally ended. But it was not so; this meant that none of them (the current generation) would ever return home. They would never see their homeland again. What a devastating blow that was. But think for a moment; that was nothing more than what they deserved for being disobedient in the first place. It is a fact that God has a plan for us. And God will ultimately give us a glorious future. The one thing we must remember is, as we walk the pathway to Christ, enduring hardships, disappointments, and heartaches that the best growth comes through persevering through the trials and not entirely escaping them. We will find unspeakable joy when we learn to persevere. Don't expect that you will not be punished for disobedience. It may not happen immediately, but rest assured, punishment is coming.

Here is the best way to uncover a false prophet: if they proclaim or declare something that does not come to pass or come true, you know they are untrue. There is no "oops" or "I made a mistake; what I meant to say was." No, you lied,

---

6. https://www.biblegateway.com/passage/?search=Jeremiah+29%3A11&version=NKJV

7. https://www.biblegateway.com/passage/?search=Jeremiah+29%3A7+&version=NKJV

you false prophet! God clearly says, "When a prophet speaks in the name of the LORD, if the word does not come to pass or come true, that is a word that the LORD has not spoken; the prophet has spoken it presumptuously. You need not be afraid of him" (Deuteronomy 18:22 ESV[8]). So be careful when someone whispers in your ear at a church revival that you are about to get a brand-new mansion or a boatload of money! Especially if they say, you need to sow a thousand-dollar seed into their ministry. God does not need a thousand-dollar seed to bless you.

The pathway to Christ will not always be easy. There will be setbacks and heartaches. But while you are going through the tough times and you are giving up, cling on to the words of Jeremiah 29:11[9]. But be sure to cling on to it for the right reasons, not the false hope of thinking that God is going to take away the suffering because of who you are, but, in the truth of His gospel, that He will give you hope in the midst of it all. The pathway can be suitable, and it can be prosperous. If you are obedient, the *Pathway to Christ* holds a great future.

---

8. https://www.biblegateway.com/passage/?search=Deuteronomy+18%3A22+&version=ESV

9. https://www.biblegateway.com/passage/?search=Jeremiah+29%3A11&version=NKJV

Pathway to Christ: Quiz

1. What does John 14:6 say?

2. What does Jeremiah 29:11 say?

3. Why did God punish the Israelites?

4. What nation did God use to punish the Israelites?

5. Name the false prophet that Jeremiah confronted.

6. How many years did the false prophet say the Israelites would be free?

7. How many years did God say the Israelites would be free?

8. Where is it found, "When a prophet speaks in the name of the LORD, if the word does not come to pass or come true, that is a word that the LORD has not spoken; the prophet has spoken it presumptuously. You need not be afraid of him"?

9. Why isn't the pathway to Christ easy?

10. Have you decided your pathway to Christ?

Notes to Self:

Sinner's Prayer

That if you confess with your mouth the Lord Jesus and believe in your heart that God has raised Him from the dead, you will be saved. ¹⁰For with the heart one believes unto righteousness,

and with the mouth confession is made unto salvation

(Romans 10:9-10 NKJV)

How often have you heard about the sinner's prayer? I used to hear about the sinner's prayer whenever we had a visiting preacher, evangelist, or prophet. After they got through preaching and ministering, they would offer prayer for those who had not been saved. In other words, it was "alter call time," after the alter call was made, a few were convicted by the word and felt compelled to come up for prayer or even give their life to Christ.

At this time, the speaker would tell those who had come forward to repeat the "sinner's prayer." Let me explain my belief in the sinner's prayer; it is a prayer to God for those who understand that they are sinners and need saving and a Savior. Just repeating a sinner's prayer will not accomplish anything on its own. A proper heart-felt sinner's prayer only represents what the person knows, understands, and believes about their sin and their need for salvation.

What is the first aspect of a sinner's prayer? It is to understand that we are all sinners. The Bible says, "For all have sinned, and come short of the glory of God" (Romans 3:23 KJV[1]). Paul said, "As it is written, there is none righteous, no, not one." The Bible illustrates that we are all sinners in need of mercy and forgiveness from the Father, "he saves us, not because of works done by us in righteousness, but according to his mercy, by washing of regeneration and renewal of the Holy Spirit, 6 whom he poured out on us richly through Jesus Christ our Savior, 7 so that being justified by his grace we might become heirs according to the hope of eternal life" (Titus 3:5-7 ESV[2]). We deserve eternal punishment because of our sins, "And these will go away into eternal punishment, but the righteous into eternal life" (Matthew 25:46 ESV[3]). The

---

1. https://www.biblegateway.com/passage/?search=Romans+3%3A23+&version=KJV

2. https://www.biblegateway.com/passage/?search=Titus+3%3A5-7+&version=ESV

sinner's prayer, instead of judgment, is a plea for grace. Instead of wrath, it is a request for mercy.

Knowing what God has done to remedy our lost and sinful condition is the second aspect of the sinner's prayer, "In the beginning was the Word, and the Word was with God, and the Word was God. 14 And the Word became flesh and dwelt among us, and we have seen his glory, glory as of the only Son from the Father, full of grace and truth" (John 1:1, 14 ESV[4]). In the Person of Jesus Christ, God took on flesh and became human. Jesus taught us the truth about God and lived sinless and righteous lives. He did not sin, and no one could prove that he did, "Which one of you convicts me of sin? If I tell the truth, why do you not believe me?" (John 8:46[5]). "For our sake he made him to be sin who knew no sin so that in him we might become the righteousness of God" (2 Corinthians 5:21 ESV[6]). Jesus rising from the dead was proof of His victory over sin, death, and hell, "He disarmed the rulers and authorities and put them to open shame, by triumphing over them in him" (Colossians 2:15 ESV[7]) (cf. 1 Corinthians 15 ESV[8]).

We can now have our sins forgiven and be promised an eternal home in heaven just by placing our faith in Christ Jesus because He died in our place, and He rose from the dead for the redemption of our sins. It all starts with us confessing and then believing that we are saved "because, if you confess with your mouth that Jesus is Lord and believe in your heart that God raised him from the dead, you will be saved. 10 For with the heart one believes and is justified, and with the mouth, one confesses and is saved" (Romans 10:9-10 ESV[9]). Paul declared, "For it is by grace you have been saved through faith. And this is not your own doing; it is the gift of God" (Ephesians 2:8 ESV[10]).

---

3. https://www.biblegateway.com/passage/?search=Matthew+25%3A46+&version=ESV

4. https://www.biblegateway.com/passage/?search=John+1%3A1%2C+14++&version=ESV

5. https://www.biblegateway.com/passage/?search=John+8%3A46&version=ESV

6. https://www.biblegateway.com/passage/?search=2+Corinthians+5%3A21&version=ESV

7. https://www.biblegateway.com/passage/?search=Colossians+2%3A15+&version=ESV

8. https://www.biblegateway.com/passage/?search=1Corinthians+15&version=ESV

9. https://www.biblegateway.com/passage/?search=Romans+10%3A9-10+&version=ESV

10. https://www.biblegateway.com/passage/?search=Ephesians+2%3A8+&version=ESV

Reciting the sinner's prayer is simply a way of declaring to God that you are, one, a sinner and two, that you confess and repent of your sins and three, believe that Jesus is the Christ, the Son of God who died on a cross, was buried and on the third day God raised Him. And we, too, can be raised with Him.

In receiving salvation, there are no "magical words," and it is only by your faith in Christ's death and resurrection that you can be saved. If you truly understand that you are a sinner in need of a Savior and are ready to say yes to Jesus today, then pray this prayer with me.

Dear Heavenly Father, I come to You admitting I am a sinner who needs rescuing. Right now, I choose to turn away from my sin and ask You to cleanse me of all unrighteousness. I believe Your Son Christ Jesus died on the cross to remove my sins. I also believe that He rose again from the dead on the third day so that I might be forgiven of my sins and made righteous through faith in Him. I call upon the name of Christ Jesus and confess Him to my Lord and Savior of my life. Jesus, I say yes to You, and I choose to follow You and ask You to fill me with the power of the Holy Spirit. I declare that right now, I am a child of God. I am from sin and full of the righteousness of God. I am saved in the name of Jesus. Amen.

If you prayed this prayer and said yes to receive Jesus Christ as your Lord and Savior, I welcome you to the family of God. From this moment on, start learning more about how to live a life of faith by finding a good Holy Spirit-filled, Bible-taught church to grow in your faith as you walk the pathway to Christ.

Notes to Self:

Saved

Then he brought them out and said, "Sirs, what must I do to be saved?

(Acts 16:30 ESV)

What can I do to be saved? What does it mean to be saved? We will attempt to address these two questions in this section of our workbook. "Being saved" is a phrase used often in the Christian faith. It is one of the most important questions one can ask in life. It is a simple yet profound question that certainly needs to be answered. You can research different dictionaries to find an adequate answer to your desired curiosity. But to truly understand what it means to be saved, you must dig out your Bible.

What can I do to be saved?

What is the process of being saved? Is there a secret code or handshake? Are there certain acts one must do to be saved? The one thing that the Bible talks about is where we will spend eternity after our life is over in this world. And being saved has much to do with where we will spend eternity. Is there any other issue more important than where our eternal destiny will be? Nope! What is abundantly clear is that the Bible talks about how a person can be saved.

While the apostle Paul and Silas were in jail in Philippi, a Jailer asked the very question many are asking today, "Sirs, what must I do to be saved?" (Acts 16:30[1] ESV). Their response was simple and instant, "Believe in the Lord Jesus, and you will be saved" (Acts 16:31[2]). Wait, that's it? Do you mean to tell me we don't have to join a secret society? Nope! The Bible says that we are all infected with sin because of Adam, and as a result of his sin, we are all sinful, "for all have sinned and fall short of the glory of God" (Romans 3:23 ESV[3]). We are all born in sin, "Behold, I was brought forth in iniquity, and in sin did my mother conceive me" (Psalms 51:5 ESV[4]). My father would say that babies are beautiful

---

1. https://www.biblegateway.com/passage/?search=Acts+16%3A30&version=ESV

2. https://www.biblegateway.com/passage/?search=Acts+16%3A31&version=ESV

3. https://www.biblegateway.com/passage/?search=Romans+3%3A23&version=ESV

4. https://www.biblegateway.com/passage/?search=Psalms+51%3A5&version=ESV

bundles of sin. There is something that we do not have to teach children, and that is to lie. Ask them about the missing cookies and see what they say. "Did you eat those cookies?" They will look you in the face and say, "No." You may not believe this, but we all personally choose to sin. The Bible says, "Surely there is not a righteous man on earth who does good and never sins" (Ecclesiastes 7:20 ESV[5]), and 1 John 1:8[6] says, "If we say we have no sin, we deceive ourselves, and the truth is not in us."

What makes us unsaved? That answer is sin. Sin is unrighteousness. And it separates us from God. The punishment for sin is eternal damnation and destruction. The Bible says that "the wages of sin is death" (Romans 6:23[7] ESV). What are wages? They are payments in return for work being done. So, if you sin, it is the same as working for evil; the payment for that sin is death. It's not a price I want to pay. Nor is it a payment I want to receive.

What does it mean to be saved?

It is no secret that we all deserve the punishment for sin. It's the consequence of our physical sinful nature. Therefore, to be saved means being rescued from the eternal punishment of hell fire for sin, right along with Satan himself. The Bible says, "But the cowardly, unbelieving, abominable, murderers, sexually immoral, sorcerers, idolaters, and all liars shall have their part in the lake which burns with fire and brimstone, which is the second death" (Revelation 21:8 ESV[8]); this is called the second death simply because it will follow the first, which is life's physical death. To be rescued from this type of death should be everyone's goal in life. Sadly, it is not. To get an accurate and graphic portrayal of hell, you must read Revelation 14:9-11[9] NKJV.

God truly wants to save everyone. But He will not force His love or will upon anyone. To prove His love for humankind, He gave His only Son, Jesus Christ, to die and to sacrifice His life for us. Because of His death, burial, and

---

5. https://www.biblegateway.com/passage/?search=Ecclesiastes+7%3A20&version=ESV

6. https://www.biblegateway.com/passage/?search=1+John+1%3A8+&version=ESV

7. https://www.biblegateway.com/passage/?search=Romans+6%3A23&version=ESV

8. https://www.biblegateway.com/passage/?search=Revelation+21%3A8&version=ESV

9. https://www.biblegateway.com/passage/?search=Rev+14%3A9-11&version=NKJV

resurrection, our sins are forgiven when we believe, confess, and repent. We are then baptized into Jesus. God promises that once we do this, we will receive "the gift of eternal life" (Romans 6:23[10] NKJV). Let me share how John puts it, "And this is the testimony: that God has given us eternal life, and this life is in His Son. 12 He who has the Son has life; he who does not have the Son of God does not have life" (1 John 5:11-12 NKJV[11]). Can it be any simpler? I think not. You can have eternal life through Christ Jesus. It's a gift. This is what it means to be saved. We are saved (rescued) from eternal separation from God into outer darkness filled with pain and misery, tormented in the flames of an unquenchable fire. You don't have to experience this punishment; no one does. It is a choice that we make of our own free will. The Bible is filled with thousands of promises. One of the promises God makes is the very one I do not want to come to pass. Because we are guilty of sin, He promises eternal damnation in Hell. Listen, God is merciful, but sin will be punished.

What do I need to do to be saved?

Finally, we can get to the most essential part of our lesson: *what you need to do to be saved*. Okay, here is what you need to do, and this is something that anyone can do if they want to be saved. It does not get any easier than this. God has already done the work for you, "For God so loved the world, that He gave His only begotten (Greek translation *monogenes*: "One and Only," "Only") Son, that whoever believes in Him should not perish but have everlasting life" (John 3:16 NKJV[12]).

What you can do. (Romans 10:9-10[13])

"Confess with your mouth the Lord Jesus (v.9)

Believe in your heart that God raised Him from the dead (v.10). You will be saved. It is with the heart that one believes in righteousness. And it is with the

---

10. https://www.biblegateway.com/passage/?search=Romans+6%3A23&version=NKJV

11. https://www.biblegateway.com/passage/?search=1+John+5%3A11%E2%80%9312&version=NKJV

12. https://www.biblegateway.com/passage/?search=John+3%3A16&version=NKJV

13. https://www.biblegateway.com/passage/?search=Romans+10%3A9-10&version=NKJV

mouth that confession is made unto salvation." That is all you need to do to be saved. This is the true Pathway to Christ.

Saved: Quiz

1. What does it mean to be saved?

2. What are the wages (payment) for sin?

3. Are you a sinner?

4. Do you believe that Jesus is the Son of God?

5. Do you believe that Jesus was crucified?

6. Do you believe that Jesus died?

7. Do you believe God raised Jesus from the dead on the third day?

8. Are you ready to confess and repent of your sins?

9. Would you like to accept Jesus into your heart?

10. Are you ready to receive Christ as your Lord and Savior?

Pray this prayer: "Dear Heavenly Father, I come to You admitting that I am a sinner in need of rescuing. Right now, I choose to turn away from my sin and ask You to cleanse me of all unrighteousness. I believe Your Son Christ Jesus died on the cross to remove my sins. I also believe that He rose again from the dead on the third day so that I might be forgiven of my sins and made righteous through faith in Him. I call upon the name of Christ Jesus and confess Him to my Lord and Savior of my life. Jesus, I say yes to You, and I choose to follow You and ask You to fill me with the power of the Holy Spirit. I declare that right now, I am a child of God. I am from sin and full of the righteousness of God. I am saved in the name of Jesus. Amen". If you prayed this prayer and said yes to receive Jesus Christ as your Lord and Savior, I welcome you to the family of God. From this moment on, start learning more about how to live a life of faith by finding a good Holy Spirit-filled, Bible-taught church to grow in your faith as you walk the pathway to Christ. I would love to hear from you.

Write to me, share your story of faith, and let me know that you said yes to Jesus today at <u>lifeswordministry@gmail.com</u>.

Notes to Self

Scriptural References

Abominations, 61 occurrences:

Lev. 18:26-27 (2 times), Lev. 18:29, Deut. 18:9, Deut. 18:12, Deut. 20:18, Deut. 32:16, 1 Ki. 14:24, 2 Ki. 16:3, 2 Ki. 21:2, 2 Ki. 21:11, 2 Chr. 28:3, 2 Chr. 33:2, 2 Chr. 34:33, 2 Chr. 36:8, 2 Chr. 36:14, Ezr. 9:1, Ezr. 9:11, Ezr. 9:14, Prov. 26:25, Jer. 7:10, Jer. 44:22, Ez. 5:9, Ez. 5:11, Ez. 6:9, Ez. 6:11, Ez. 7:3-4 (2x), Ez. 7:8-9 (2x), Ez. 7:20, Ez. 8:6 (2x), Ez. 8:9, Ez. 8:13, Ez. 8:15, Ez. 8:17, Ez. 9:4, Ez. 11:18, Ez. 11:21, Ez. 12:16, Ez. 14:6, Ez. 16:2, Ez. 16:22, Ez. 16:36, Ez. 16:43, Ez. 16:47, Ez. 16:51 (2x), Ez. 16:58, Ez. 18:13, Ez. 18:24, Ez. 20:4, Ez. 22:2, Ez. 23:36, Ez. 33:29, Ez. 36:31, Ez. 43:8, Ez. 44:6-7 (2x), Ez. 44:13

Abomination, 52 occurrences:

Gen. 43:32, Gen. 46:34, Exo. 8:26 (2 times), Lev. 18:22, Lev. 20:13, Deut. 7:25-26 (2x), Deut. 12:31, Deut. 13:14, Deut. 17:1, Deut. 17:4, Deut. 18:12, Deut. 22:5, Deut. 23:18, Deut. 24:4, Deut. 25:16, Deut. 27:15, 2 Ki. 23:13, Psa. 88:8, Prob. 3:32, Prob. 6:16, Prob. 8:7, Prob. 11:1, Prob. 11:20, Prob. 12:22, Prob. 13:19, Prob. 15:8-9 (2x), Prob. 15:26, Prob. 16:5, Prob. 16:12, Prob. 17:15, Prob. 20:10, Prob. 20:23, Prob. 21:27, Prob. 28:9 (2x), Prob. 29:27 (2x), Isa. 1:13, Isa. 41:24, Isa. 44:19, Jer. 2:7, Jer. 6:15, Jer. 8:12, Jer. 32:35, Ez. 16:50, Ez. 18:12, Ez. 22:11, Ez. 33:26, Mal. 2:11

Abominable, 4 occurrences:

Lev. 18:30, Deut. 14:3, Jer. 16:18, Jer. 44:4

N.T. References: Matt. 24:15, Lk. 16:14-15 (2 times), Rev. 21:27, Rev. 17:4-5 (2x)

Faith and Wisdom:

Hebrews 11; John 10:10; Romans 12:2; 1 Corinthians 2:5-10, 14; 13:12; James 1:2-4

Heaven:

Deuteronomy 26:15; 1 King 8:30; 2 Chronicles 30:27; Job 22:12; Psalms 73:25; 123:1; Isaiah 66:1 Luke 11:2; Acts 7:49

Heavens:

Genesis 1:1; 1 Chronicles 16:26 Psalms 102:25; Proverbs 8:27; Isaiah 40:22; 42:5; 45:12; Jeremiah 32:17

Hell:

Matthew 25:41

Luke 16:24

New Creation:

2 Corinthians 5:17

Partiality/Favoritism:

James 2:1-13

Paul's Conversion:

Acts 9

Salvation:

Romans 10:9-10; Philippians 3:4-11

Summary of Paul's Sufferings:

2 Corinthians 11:21-33

The Cleansing of the Temple:

John 2:13-22

The Crucifixion of Christ:

Matthew 27

The Day of Pentecost:

Acts 2

The Day of Pentecost:

Act 2

The First Sin:

Genesis 3

The Five "I Wills of Satan":

Isaiah 14:13-14

The Jailers Conversion:

Act 16:25-34

The Stoning of Stephen:

Acts 6 and 7

The Trinity (Godhead):

Genesis 1:1, 26; 3:22; 11:7; Isaiah 6:8, 48:16, 61:1; Matthew 3:16-17, 28:19; 2 Corinthians 13:14

The Way:

John 14:6

Trials and Joy:

1 Peter 1:6-9

Recommended Resources

Destruction and Rebuilding of the Temple:

Retrieved from https://www.bibleodyssey.org/en/places/related-articles/destruction-and-reconstruction-of-the-temple.aspx

Jehovah's Witness on Tongues:

Retrieved from https://www.jw.org/en/bible-teachings/questions/speaking-in-tongues/

Ekklesia:

Thayer and Smith. (1999). "Greek Lexicon entry for Ekklesia". "The NAS New Testament Greek Lexicon[1]".

Examination of Acts 2:38:

Retrieved from https://carm.org/baptism-and-acts-238

Fairchild, M. (2018) "Top Books About Heaven" ThoughtCo. Retrieved from https://www.thoughtco.com/top-books-about-heaven-700313

Five Pillars of Islam:

Retrieved from http://www.islam101.com/dawah/pillars.html

Four Views on Hell:

Retrieved from https://www.christianbook.com/four-views-on-hell/john-walvoord/9780310212683/pd/21268?event=AFF&p=1011693&

Heaven:

---

1. http://www.biblestudytools.com/lexicons/greek/nas/

Heaven. (n.d.) *American Heritage® Dictionary of the English Language, Fifth Edition.*   (2011).   Retrieved   April   5,   2019   from https://www.thefreedictionary.com/heaven

Pew Research Center: Most Americans Believe in Heaven

Retrieved   from   https://www.pewforum.org/2015/11/03/u-s-public-becoming-less-religious/

Roman Catholic Church:

Retrieved from The Gospel According to Rome: Comparing Catholic Tradition and The Word of God by James McCarthy[2])

Salvation:

The New Dictionary of Cultural Literacy, Third Edition. Retrieved from https://www.dictionary.com/browse/salvation

Smith, W. (1901) Sanhedrin:

Retrieved   from   https://www.biblestudytools.com/dictionaries/ smiths-bible-dictionary/sanhedrin.html

The Holy Spirit:

Retrieved from The Holy Spirit by Charles Ryrie[3]

72 Virgins:

Retrieved   from   http://www.aviperry.org/political-blogs/where-did-the-notion-of-72-virgins-in-islamic-paradise-come-from

---

2. https://www.christianbook.com/Christian/Books/product?event=AFF&p=1011693&item_no=71077

3. https://www.christianbook.com/Christian/Books/product?event=AFF&p=1011693&item_no=35785

Acknowledgments

First and foremost, before I start my shout-outs, I want to thank God! I have not always been what one would consider a model Christian all of the time. But God kept me. I am so glad that God is a God of a second chance. And in my case. I've lost count of how many times.

I have been battling with the thought of writing for many years, even while attending college. Many of my professors suggested that I use the gift that God has blessed me with and write. I never really considered myself a serious writer, but here I am. Lord, I thank you.

Now, on to the shoutouts. Lord, please do not allow me to forget anyone! To the love of my life for the rest of my life, my friend, my rib, my encouragement, my everything, and most importantly, my wife, Christine. Thank you so much for allowing me to be me. If it were not for you, I don't think I would be writing or doing many of the exciting things I am now doing, and I don't think I would even attempt them. You bring the jiggy back into my life. Even though we both knew initially, you were attracted to me because you thought I was Will Smith's older brother! I love you dearly!

To my parents, Bishop Henry and Lady Lola Mitchell. I can't thank you enough for being the spiritual example you have been in my life. Because of how you raised me, I am who I am today. Your love and countless prayers have protected me and guided my entire life.

To my brother Derrick Sr. and Jacqueline's wife (a true-blue sister). Thank you for being there when I needed to escape and chill. Thanks for all the tough talks and for knowing that life is "Incredible" no matter what.

To my three wonderful children (Ashlyn, Terrell, Deja) and my three fabulous grandchildren (Serenity, Saige, and Cason), Ashlyn, you are indeed your daddy through and through. I am so proud of you and how you have grown up to be a wonderful mother and wife to Chuck (a great husband). God is using you to bless the world through your gifts and talents. You have not allowed disappointment and betrayal to hinder God's designed purpose in your life. You have risen out of the ashes of traditional dogma to shine bright in the darkness and have helped other women and wives find their way out. Y'all don't know? You better ask somebody (www.spicedwife.com). You and Chuck have given me some exceptional grandchildren. I love you dearly. To my son Anthony "Terrell," you are my pride and joy! And the prince of the kingdom (whatever that is). I am incredibly proud to see how you have been molded into the kind of man I knew was trying to be birthed out of that rigid and stubborn cocoon. And a real man emerged that any woman would be proud and happy to have in her life (especially since you can do her wig). I thank God for you and the gifts that He has blessed you with. Never stop moving upwards! Your past steps prove that you are a fighter and a winner. Last but certainly not least! My Deja "Bug," you are indeed my miracle baby. My shy one! God is crafting your life wonderfully and turning you into such a beautiful young woman. I can hardly wait to see all that you will accomplish. I love you all so very much,

Daddy

To my dearest and most treasured friends, Robert Edwards R.I.P., the late Bishop Antoine Bradford, Rosemary Bradford, Antoine Bradford IV (Way to go BOUY), and Jeremy Bradford, Pastor "JP" and April Prothro, Mimi (Zumba Queen) Wright, Sean Slaughter, Erroll Williams, Kadell Felton, Sr., the Benson's, Willie and Marva Jones, and to *all* my LGC boy's like my little brotha, "IKE" Walker, all you that I could not list from the Living Gospel Church fellowship; you all have especially touched my life. To my GSC (Good Samaritan Church) family (like Fred "Bumpy" Byers), where you lack in number, you make up in loyalty and love!

A special thank you to those who took the time out of their busy schedule to endorse my book: Professor Rick Epps, Jessica Janniere, Greg (Big Dreamer) Walker, and Dr. Roseanna Roman. And to my editor, Dani Rene. You are the best! Without you, this could not have been accomplished. I am forever in your debt because that's how long we will work together!

To the hosts of family and friends, thank you for sharing my life. I dedicate this to you all!

A Message to My Readers:

Pathway to Christ is a simple workbook for learning simple fundamentals of walking a pathway of godliness and living a life by faith. Thank you for your prayers, love, and support. If you would like to sow into this ministry, you can do so by going to PayPal.me/lifeswordministry[1]

#liveinhopeandchange #lifeswordministry #pathwaytochrist

---

1. https://www.paypal.me/Lifeswordministry

About the Author

Pastor Malachi was born and raised in San Diego, California. Malachi modeled and acted on several local theatrical shows, movies, and TV commercials for ten years.

His other career endeavors include working as an employee for the City of San Diego. He was forced into early retirement after a terrible on-the-job vehicle accident, which launched him into his entrepreneurship journey.

Pastor Malachi received his bachelor's and master's degree in Christian Studies with an Emphasis in Leadership from Grand Canyon University, AZ. His ministry endeavors include becoming a licensed and ordained minister in 1984, Youth Leader from 1998-2008, then Youth Pastor from 2008-2014, and has been the Co-Pastor at Good Samaritan Church of San Diego alongside his brother, who is currently the Assistant Pastor to their father and mother, Senior Pastor Bishop Henry Mitchell, Jr. and Lady Lola Mitchell.

God placed a vision in Malachi after he retired from the City of San Diego, where he also became the founder of "The Spoken Word Ministries." Recently, God moved upon him to rename it "Life's WORD Ministry" in 2017.

In 2011, Pastor Malachi became Facebook friends with Christine via LegalShield (formerly known as Pre-Paid Legal). After meeting in person in August of 2016 at a bonfire in San Diego (arranged by Pastor Malachi), Pastor Malachi and Christine realized that God had a greater divine purpose for their lives. In October of 2017, they were united as husband and wife. Between the two of them, they have seven children and three grandchildren.

Together, their mission is to reach, teach, empower, encourage, uplift, and motivate people of all ages. They want to help in the healing process of battered mothers and children and reconnect children with their absent fathers. They endeavor to correct many of the societal mistakes that have caused an increase in homeless men, women, and children and to help rebuild family structure. One of their many goals is to help those less fortunate regain a sense of appreciation for life again through many of their self-awareness workshops. The core value of their ministry is founded on Biblical principles: reclaiming, rebuilding, and restoring people's trust and helping them to **Live** in **Hope** and **Change**.

Writing has always been Malachi's passion, but he has never pursued it seriously. Training and teaching are a true calling in his life, and he loves to do so, so writing a Christian workbook is a dream come true.

Quiz Answers

In the Beginning:

1. Paul.

2. "If you confess with your mouth that Jesus is Lord...you will be saved".

3. Grace, Gift, Faith, Speak.

4. Salvation or They are saved.

5. That if you confess with your mouth the Lord Jesus and believe in your heart that God had raised Him from the dead, you will be saved. 10. For with the heart one believes unto righteousness, and with the mouth, confession is made unto salvation.

6. Open answer

7. Paul.

8. Tarsus.

9. Damascus. To round up Christians to kill.

10. Events in Paul's life:

- The witnessing of Stephen's stoning

- Received three years of personal teaching Jesus while living in Arabia

- Resurrected at least one person from the dead

- Carried out at least five evangelistic journeys

- Visited more than 50 cities

- Five times received thirty-nine stripes

- Beaten three times with rods

- Stoned once

- Shipwrecked three times

- Was Robbed

- Bitten by a snake

- Left out in the cold, naked, thirsty, and hungry

- Let down a wall in a basket to escape the governor under Aretas, the king

- Preached the gospel to Emperor Caesar and his entire household

- Wrote no less than fourteen books (epistles/letters) of the Bible (no other author can say that)

- Trained and instructed other evangelists and preachers of the gospel (John Mark and Timothy)

- He endured more than five years in prison

In the Middle:

1. a. The Joy the World Gives Is Not the Same Joy That God Gives.

b. God's Joy Cannot Be Taken Away.

c. You Have to Grab onto God's Joy.

2. No. At times, they may seem to be amplified.

3. He encouraged and instructed them to have faith in their trials so that their faith could develop perseverance.

4. Five things Peter was known for:

a. Being one of Jesus' disciples.

b. The one called the "Rock."

c. Walking on water.

d. Cutting off a man's ear in the Garden of Gethsemane.

e. Denying Christ three times.

5. Be strong and courageous. Do not be afraid or terrified because of them, for the Lord your God goes with you; he will never leave you nor forsake you.

6. True joy comes in your walk of faith.

7. Joy, Lord, Strength.

8. Joy.

9. Persecuted.

10. Grab onto it.

What Faith, Now Faith

1. What is one of the most important elements in a person's life?

2. What are the two aspects of faith?

a. Faith.

b. You must believe.

3. Even the demons believe and shudder.

4. "For by *grace* you have been saved through faith. And this is not your own doing; it is the gift of God, not a result of works, as that no one may boast" (Ephesians 2:8-9[1] ESV).

5. It is the gift of God.

---

1. https://www.biblegateway.com/passage/?search=Ephesians+2%3A8-9&version=ESV

6. Faith.

7. Pure joy.

8. By drawing closer to God through praying and studying His Word.

9. Be anxious for nothing, but in everything by prayer and supplication, with thanksgiving, let your requests, be made known to God; and the peace of God, which surpasses all understanding, will guard your hearts and minds through Christ Jesus.

10. a. By confessing our sins (John 1:7[2] NKJV; 1 John 1:9[3] NKJV).

b. By seeking Him (Ps. 27:8[4] NKJV; Isa. 55:6[5] NKJV).

c. By Surrendering to Him (Gal. 3:3[6] NKJV; Col 2:6[7] NKJV; Rom. 12:1[8] NKJV).

New Creation:

1. Therefore, if anyone *is* in Christ, he *is* a new creation; old things have passed away; behold, all things have become new.

2. Open Answer.

3. Nature, Nailed, Cross, Jesus.

4. Lovers of sin. b. Natural pride. c. Passions. d. Bad habits. e. Unnatural affections.

f. Reliance of works.

2. https://www.biblegateway.com/passage/?search=John+1%3A7&version=NKJV

3. https://www.biblegateway.com/passage/?search=1+John+1%3A9&version=NKJV

4. https://www.biblegateway.com/passage/?search=Ps.+27%3A8&version=NKJV

5. https://www.biblegateway.com/passage/?search=Isa.+55%3A6&version=NKJV

6. https://www.biblegateway.com/passage/?search=Gal.+3%3A3&version=NKJV

7. https://www.biblegateway.com/passage/?search=Col+2%3A6&version=NKJV

8. https://www.biblegateway.com/passage/?search=Rom.+12%3A1&version=NKJV

5. Life. Dead.

6. 1 Corinthians 15:31[9]

7. If you have been set free from sin, say so by testifying what God has done in your life.

8. True.

9. False.

10. Creation.

Be the Church:

1. Peter.

2. Act 2.

3. "an assembly" or better yet, "called-out, from the world for God".

4. False.

5. False.

6. False.

7. True.

8. 120

9. By sacrificially giving your all to and for Christ.

10. Open answer.

The Holy Spirit:

1. Spirit.

---

9. https://www.biblegateway.com/passage/?search=1+Corinthians+15%3A31&version=NKJV

2. God the Father. God the Son. God the Holy Spirit.

3. Comforter / Counselor / Helper / Advocate / Intercessor / Author / The Lord / Christ / Witness

4. The Book of the Holy Spirit.

5. By the Holy Spirit.

6. The Holy Spirit.

7. They were first cousins.

8. Elizabeth.

9. "Go ye therefore, and make disciples of all the nations, baptizing them into the name of the Father, and of the Son and of the Holy Spirit".

10. Open answer.

Tongues:

1. In the Book of Acts (Act 2:1-4 NIV[10])

2. Languages.

3. False.

4. False.

5. What are two reasons mentioned that the Holy Spirit was given?

a. to edify the Body of Christ.

b. to glorify God.

6. "For by grace are ye saved through faith; and that not of yourselves: *it is* the gift of God"

7. a. Private prayer language.

---

10. https://www.biblegateway.com/passage/?search=Acts+2%3A1-4&version=NIV

b. Tongue that is interpreted.

c. Tongue of missionary context.

8. What is the importance of speaking in tongues?

9. The believe that tongues have ceased.

10. Open answer.

Heaven:

1. Open answer.

2. God.

3. Genesis 1:1.

4. John 14:2

5. Through Jesus.

6. In Heaven.

7. It is the dwelling place of God. A place of fellowship and eternal joy.

8. Wherever God is.

9. 276 times.

10. To one day see God face to face in our new home, heaven.

Hell:

1. Hell.

2. Gehenna.

3. "a star that had fallen from the sky to earth".

4. Isaiah 14:13-14

a. I will ascend into heaven.

b. I will exalt my throne above the stars of God.

c. I will sit also upon the mount of the congregation.

d. I will ascend above the heights of the clouds.

e. I will be like the Most High.

5. a. P – Position.

b. R – Rule.

c. I – Idolized.

d. D – Dominion.

e. E – Equality.

6. For Satan and those angels that rebelled against God.

7. Open answer.

8. For sinning. Turning their backs on God. Rejecting Him.

9. Salvation/Jesus Christ.

10. Being cast into the lake of fire.

Sin:

1. Sin is a transgression against the laws of God.

2. Hamartiology.

3. Lucifer.

4. Deceiving.

5. Their spiritual eyes came open. They spiritually died.

6. They were kicked out of the garden.

7. A snake.

8. a. Proud look.

b. Lying tongue.

c. Murder.

d. Heart that devises wicked.

e. Feet that are swift in running to evil.

f. One who sows discord among brethren.

9. All who behave unrighteous.

10. [9]that if you confess with your mouth the Lord Jesus and believe in your heart that God has raised Him from the dead, you will be saved. [10]For with the heart one believes unto righteousness, and with the mouth, confession is made unto salvation.

Salvation:

1. "Preservation or deliverance from harm, ruin, or loss".

2. Jesus.

3. a. First, you must hear the good news of Christ Jesus, His crucifixion, His death and burial, and His resurrection.

b. Second, you must believe and fully put your trust in Jesus as your Lord and Savior (Romans 10:10[11]), and not be ashamed what He did for you by forgiving you from you transgressions.

4. a. The Why.

b. The Who.

c. The How.

5. What are the Five Pillars of Islam?

---

11. https://www.biblegateway.com/passage/?search=Romans+10%3A10&version=ESV

a. Shahada

b. Prayer

c. Fasting

d. Alms-giving of charity

e. Pilgrimage

6. Two things that distinguish the Christian faith from other religions are:

a. One, it's not a religion; it's a relationship with Christ.

b. two, there are no steps that you must follow to receive salvation.

7. False.

8. True.

9. False.

10. "For by grace you have been saved through faith. And this is not your own doing; it is the gift of God" (Ephesians 2:8 ESV[12]).

Baptism:

1. To immerse in water.

2. baptism is an outward, not an inward, proclamation of the conversion that takes place on the inside.

3. John baptized with water unto repentance.

4. With the Holy Ghost and with fire.

5. No. Baptism is not what saves us. Baptism is not part of salvation, and baptism is not necessary for salvation. Baptism is what someone does who is already saved.

---

12. https://www.biblegateway.com/passage/?search=Ephesians+2%3A8+&version=ESV

6. Baptism.

7. The gospel: the resurrection of Christ.

8. Baptism.

9. True.

10. Open answer.

Pathway to Christ:

1. Jesus said to him, "I am the way, the truth, and the life. No one comes to the Father except through me."

2. For I know the plans I have for you,' says the Lord, 'plans for well-being and not for trouble, to give you a future and a hope.

3. The Israelites had been exiled as a punishment for their disobedience.

4. Babylon.

5. Hananiah.

6. Two years.

7. Seventy years.

8. Deuteronomy 18:22.

9. There will be setbacks and heartaches.

10. Open answer.

Don't miss out!

Visit the website below and you can sign up to receive emails whenever Malachi Mitchell publishes a new book. There's no charge and no obligation.

https://books2read.com/r/B-A-PMKGB-FRTAD

BOOKS 2 READ

Connecting independent readers to independent writers.